W0018197

SAGE was founded in 1965 by Sara Miller McCune to support the dissemination of usable knowledge by publishing innovative and high-quality research and teaching content. Today, we publish over 900 journals, including those of more than 400 learned societies, more than 800 new books per year, and a growing range of library products including archives, data, case studies, reports, and video. SAGE remains majority-owned by our founder, and after Sara's lifetime will become owned by a charitable trust that secures our continued independence.

Los Angeles | London | New Delhi | Singapore | Washington DC | Melbourne

INDIA ON THE
WESTERN SCREEN

INDIA ON THE WESTERN SCREEN

IMAGING A COUNTRY IN FILM, TV, AND DIGITAL MEDIA

ANANDA MITRA

Los Angeles I London I New Delhi
Singapore I Washington DC I Melbourne

Copyright © Ananda Mitra, 2016

All rights reserved. No part of this book may be reproduced or utilized in any form or by any means, electronic or mechanical, including photocopying, recording or by any information storage or retrieval system, without permission in writing from the publisher.

First published in 2016 by

SAGE Publications India Pvt Ltd
B1/I-1 Mohan Cooperative Industrial Area
Mathura Road, New Delhi 110 044, India
www.sagepub.in

SAGE Publications Inc
2455 Teller Road
Thousand Oaks, California 91320, USA

SAGE Publications Ltd
1 Oliver's Yard, 55 City Road
London EC1Y 1SP, United Kingdom

SAGE Publications Asia-Pacific Pte Ltd
3 Church Street
#10-04 Samsung Hub
Singapore 049483

Published by Vivek Mehra for SAGE Publications India Pvt Ltd, typeset in Minion Pro 11/13 pts by Zaza Eunice, Hosur, Tamil Nadu, India and printed at Chaman Enterprises, New Delhi.

Library of Congress Cataloging-in-Publication Data

Names: Mitra, Ananda, author.
Title: India on the Western screen : imaging a country in film, TV and
   digital media / Ananda Mitra.
Description: New Delhi ; Thousand Oaks, California : SAGE Publications, 2016.
   | Includes bibliographical references and index.
Identifiers: LCCN 2016014127 | ISBN 9789351509776 (hardback : alk. paper) |
   ISBN 9789351509783 (epub) | ISBN 9789351509769 (ebook)
Subjects: LCSH: India—In motion pictures. | India—In mass media.
Classification: LCC PN1993.5.I8 M4655 2016 | DDC 791.43/6254—dc23 LC
   record available at https://lccn.loc.gov/2016014127

ISBN: 978-93-515-0977-6 (HB)

The SAGE Team: Shambhu Sahu, Sanghamitra Patowary, Kumar Indra Mishra, and Ritu Chopra

All images used in this book (including the cover) are for representative purposes only and are solely owned by the respective copyright owners.

This book is dedicated to all who have to live a real life based on how they are shown on the screen.

Thank you for choosing a SAGE product!
If you have any comment, observation or feedback,
I would like to personally hear from you.
Please write to me at **contactceo@sagepub.in**

Vivek Mehra, Managing Director and CEO, SAGE India.

Bulk Sales

SAGE India offers special discounts
for purchase of books in bulk.
We also make available special imprints
and excerpts from our books on demand.

For orders and enquiries, write to us at

Marketing Department
SAGE Publications India Pvt Ltd
B1/I-1, Mohan Cooperative Industrial Area
Mathura Road, Post Bag 7
New Delhi 110044, India

E-mail us at **marketing@sagepub.in**

Get to know more about SAGE

Be invited to SAGE events, get on our mailing list.
Write today to **marketing@sagepub.in**

This book is also available as an e-book.

CONTENTS

LIST OF IMAGES

PREFACE

The screen is a strange term. It has many meanings and many implications. In the twenty-first century, we are surrounded by screens that bring information to us. For some, a screen, such as the viewing space of the smartphone, is so much a part of life that some municipalities have thought of creating separate walking paths for those who are glued to their smartphone screens so that people do not run into each other. Other screens are encountered from the privacy of the home to public spaces where large screens greet people. Some say that the screens of Times Square in New York can be seen from far up in space. This book is about screens; the first part of the book elaborates on screens to offer the reader a sense of what they are and how they operate in the lives of audiences.

Since screens do not operate in the absence of audiences, this book also elaborates on the different kinds of audiences that are exposed to the screens. Given that the book deals particularly with India, the audiences considered here are the ones that are relevant to India in the West. Thus, a good part of the book examines the kinds of audience, especially of Indian origin, who are found in the West and who have to interact with the larger audiences that witness India on the different screens of the West.

Finally, all these screens and audiences make up a system which we are all a part of. Consequently, what happens on the Western screen about India impacts us all, especially if one is an Indian. The book closes with the implications of the images on the screen and offers a theoretical explanation as to why Indians are treated in certain ways by the people of the West. The way India is represented on the Western screen is not merely a matter of curiosity. Instead, this book offers a sense of what to expect out of the representations when two individuals interact with each other within the social sphere created by the images. In other words, what has movies such as *Slumdog Millionaire* done to how India is perceived globally, or what does the appearance of Priyanka Chopra in the popular American crime thriller *Quantico* does to Americans thinking of Indians in America?

Image P.1. A Screenshot from *Quantico* (Season 1, Episode 5), a Show that Aired on American Network Channel ABC that Features an Indian Protagonist

Courtesy: Author.

ACKNOWLEDGMENTS

I would like to thank my wife Swati Basu for introducing me to the world of Indian programs on satellite TV and patiently watching numerous movies that are featured in this book.

I would like to thank my son Srijoy Mitra who, as a second-generation diasporic Indian in America, has shown me the challenges that he and many others face as they have to live with the images that are seen on the Western screens as discussed in this book.

I would like to thank the students in our "Immersed in India" class, who have shown me the challenges that they face when they have to negotiate their sojourn in India and that they are often influenced by the images that they have encountered on the Western screens.

Many thanks to all members of my family, my friends, and my colleagues who have to live with my oddities as I research and write.

1. INDIA ON THE WESTERN SCREEN: 20 YEARS LATER

For my book published in 1994—*India through the Western Lens*—I was motivated by a simple event that had happened in a parking lot in Edison, New Jersey, in 1992, about eight years after I had moved to the United States from India. This is a town about 50 miles away from New York City and set in the sprawling megalopolis that stretches from Washington to Boston. Some will know that Edison, for a long time, has been a dwelling place for people from India. Indeed, in a 2008 article in *The New York Times*, Joseph Berger said, "Oak Tree Road, which runs through this sprawling town of 100,000 people and into neighboring Woodbridge Township, may be America's liveliest Little India, with 400 Indian businesses that attract Indian immigrants from across the region."[1] It is in this township of Edison that I had an interesting experience. I had just parked my car in the parking lot

---

[1] http://www.nytimes.com/2008/04/27/nyregion/nyregionspecial2/27indianj.html?pagewanted=all&_r=0

of one of those nondescript apartment blocks that can be found in any American town. Walking back to my friend's place, I passed by three young Caucasian girls no more than probably 15-years old. One of them said out loud, "Go back to India." Years of training in wit and street smartness kicked in and without missing a beat or stopping to look back, I said out loud, "Go back to Europe."

This event, however, had an impact on me. I became curious about the culture that allowed such a statement to be made. It was not only that specific statement, but also similar other moments in the lives of numerous individuals from India who faced such statements, jibes, the askance, or the special treatment at Western airports; those all were of interest to me and my journey. This matter led me to look at the ways in which Western movies have portrayed India and the people of that part of the world. It resulted in the 1994 book, *India through the Western Lens*. Much has changed in the last three decades, and India and its people have been reimagined and re-represented in many different ways from what happened in films such as *Gunga Din* (1939) and *City of Joy* (1992). In the 2010s, there are many different and many more modes of representing a place and its people. Here, in 2015, I examine the new representations, the new images, and the new imaginations, and how they impact India and the people from India.

The notion of images is especially critical here. In his 1983 book, *Imagined Communities*, Benedict Anderson[2] suggests that communities are imagined around specific modes of talking about the community. He emphasizes much on the role of the printed press in allowing communities and nations to imagine themselves and invent the sense of nationalism for a particular place. Within this argument, Anderson also underscores the role of narratives that play into the imagination of the nation. These stories, often in print, allow for a group of people to band around the narrative and actualize the sense of community that is produced by the story. Sometimes these stories take on the nature of myths. Scholars such as Levi-Strauss[3] have argued that myths distil out the very

[2] Benedict Richard O'Gorman Anderson, *Imagined Communities: Reflections on the Origin and Spread of Nationalism* (Verso: London, 1983).
[3] C. Levi-Strauss, *The Structural Study of Myth. Structural Anthropology* (New York: Basic Books, 1955).

essence of a story. There are, thus, myths that make up nature of a person or an event. Consider, for instance, the story that Newton understood the notion of gravity when an apple fell on his head. Whether this story is true or not is not as much the issue as the vivid way in which it represents the person and the idea of gravity within popular culture and allows the community of physicists to explain the notion of gravity. Every community has its myths and stories that become the center around which the community can be built. Indeed, the importance of stories is also pointed out in the work of Walter Fisher[4] who argued that believable stories give meaning to the events around us.

Fisher[5] suggested that within a "narrative paradigm" of life, the human being becomes a story-telling being, where the stories allow us to make sense of the life around us. Stories remind us of who we are, what we believe in, and how we act. Within the narrative paradigm of life, it is the convincing and persuasive stories that allow us to create personal and communal identities. Thus, different scholars have pointed toward the importance of stories in the life of societies. As a corollary, I argue that knowledge of the stories about a person, community, group, or population would allow for a specific understanding of the subject of the stories.

The stories could become representations of the people. My earlier book was built on this specific premise, and I examined the stories on film to discover how India was being narrated by the Western lens. The study supported the finding that there were specific and repetitive strategies of storytelling that created a specific image of the place and its people. The leap from stories to representation is supported by other scholars such as Stuart Hall[6] who has argued that some of the stories are indeed "identity narratives" that allow for telling the story of a particular person. As a matter of fact, we all create our personal identity narratives. Some are benign, such as stating where one was born, whereas others are

---

[4] W. R. Fisher, *Human Communication as Narration: Toward a Philosophy of Reason, Value, and Action* (Columbia: University of South Carolina Press, 1987).

[5] Fisher, *Human Communication as Narration*.

[6] S. Hall, "Encoding/Decoding," in *Culture, Media, Language: Working Papers in Cultural Studies, 1972–79*, eds. Hall, D. Hobson, A. Lowe, and P. Willis (London: Hutchinson, 1980), 128–138.

complex, carefully structured, and skillfully performed identity narratives. Narratives represent the identity of a person or a group. It is, thus, possible to imagine a group or a place by knowing the narratives about them. It becomes especially powerful when the stories become connected with each other or repeat themselves, and are circulated within a popular culture over and over again. Eventually, such representations that create the image become a part of the natural and conventional way of thinking of a place. It is even truer when the representations become the only way to create the identity of a place or person. Consider, for an instance, your personal image of a place you have never been to. In most of the cases, that imagination has to be built around the way in which that identity has been created by representations of the place or person. At precisely that instant the narrative identity becomes critical because those images represent the place and produce the identity of the entity being imaged. It is, thus, useful to consider the notion of identity at this juncture to establish some of the basic principles of this book.

IDENTITY

The notion of identity is an often-discussed and closely-contested item in scholarly circles as many have considered the answer to the pressing personal question "Who am I?" This personal question can, however, be extrapolated to larger units, such as groups of people, communities, and ultimately nation states. There have been many ways of attempting to answer questions such as "What is India?" or "Who were the Knights Templars?" There could be historical treatise that is mobilized to answer such questions just as there could be discussions of politics and economics that could be used to answer such questions. One of the ways in which the question has been answered is indeed through the notion of narratives as discussed earlier. Specific stories help to create the identity narrative of a person, place, group, or nation. Consider the case of an individual when faced with the task of describing the self, a person often starts with places of origin saying this, such as, "I am from Barcelona." And then the person might go on to provide a historical narrative of the self. In doing that, the person has presented himself through a story. Such stories, in the collection, become the narratives of a group of people and, thus, present the identity of the group.

In the groundbreaking work on identity narratives, specifically in his work on the identity of people from the Caribbean, noted British scholar Stuart Hall[7] offers a way of thinking about such narratives that provide the cultural identity of people through specific historical narratives that represent the people in a dynamic way, sometimes calling into question earlier narratives of identity and representing to the world a new narrative to re-identify an entity. This process is particularly true for the people who have urgency to represent themselves, and update and modify an existing narrative of the self. Consider a person who has moved from a place of origin to a new place of adoption, as in the case of a migrant laborer or an immigrant to a new country. For such people, there are different identities connected to different places and different times. The household domestic help in an upscale home in Delhi has a narrative that connects her with another place—Bihar, Bangladesh, or West Bengal—and a narrative that is connected to being a servant in Delhi. These could be conflicting narratives, but all are built by the stories a person tells to different listeners, constantly, through the imagery of language of the stories, creating a personal identity.

This process, however, is true for entities beyond a specific person. This is true for a nation that would have specific stories associated with it. These stories become centers around which national identities are constructed. This is true for India as it is for any other place. For instance, until 2002, there was no clear image associated with India as a tourism destination for travelers from other countries. However, in 2002, the Ministry of Tourism retained the services of an advertising company, Ogilvy and Mather, to tell the story of India to a foreign audience with the purpose of creating an identity for India in the minds of tourists. This led to the well-known, "Incredible!ndia" campaign, where the visual story of India was spelled out as, "Incredible!ndia" offering a specific identity, vis-à-vis tourism, for India. The evidence suggests that this representation of India was quite effective in the

---

[7] Hall, "Encoding/Decoding," 1980.

marketing terms, and in the first year of the use of this narrative, there was a 16 percent increase in tourist traffic to India.[8] While that increase might not have been completely due to the creation of the narrative about India around the specific images and languages, it is the case that a specific story about India was manufactured through the use of the pictures and the tag line.

However, the process through which the particular story was created also points toward the need for identity narratives to be dynamic. This has been true for the institutional campaign narrative encapsulated in the Incredible!ndia campaign as some tourism industry leaders are suggesting that the campaign needs to be "revamped" since it has outlived its utility.[9] From a purely marketing and advertising perspective, this could well make sense since the goal here is to produce opportunities for the government and tourism industry to attract revenues and grow the business of tourism in India. However, the term "revamped" is strikingly close to the notion of "representation." In providing the criticism that the campaign needs to be revamped, the tourism industry is essentially asking for a new story about India that would re-image the nation providing yet another narrative identity. This is, precisely, how stories about a place can create the identity of a place. Indeed, there needs to be a stress on the plurality of identity and a reminder that people, places, communities, and nations, all possess multiple identities based on multiple stories about the entity.

MULTIPLICITY OF IDENTITIES

In the disciplines of psychology and psychiatry, the chronic and extreme multiplicity of identities that an individual might possess becomes a matter of concern in terms of the fact that the person might not be fully functional in the society, as in the case of schizophrenia. However, even for those, not diagnosed with conditions such as schizophrenia, it is not unlikely that a person would have specific and different identity narratives suitable for different audiences. This is akin to stating that we tell different stories

---

[8] http://incredibleindiacampaign.com/
[9] http://www.thesundayindian.com/en/story/'incredible-india'-campaign-need-to-be-revamped-experts/5/24856/

about ourselves to different people. The identity narratives are not necessarily deceptive, but they can certainly be strategic. Consider the case of someone who has chosen to emigrate from one place of residence to other. Such people could select how they describe themselves through the stories they select about themselves. A few stories are meant for those who know them well, other stories are meant for the strangers, and in that fashion multiple identities are produced to serve different functions. The multiplicity of identities for people is a well-known fact of the way in which people represent themselves. Indeed, in some cases, this multiplicity becomes a part of the culture and it is coded into the cultural practices. For example, some groups of people, such as those from West Bengal in India, would label people with two names. One of the names would be the "public" name, used for producing the public identity of the person, and the other is the "private" name which is often used by a more intimate circle of friends and family. A person chooses which name to use in specific circumstances and simply by the use of the name, a specific identity is created. Such multiplicity of identity can also extend to groups of people and places.

The way a place is named or described produces a specific image of the place, and places can also have multiple names which represent different aspects of that place. In some cases, they conjure up different visions of the place. The names "United States" and "America" present two different ways of thinking about the place. While the first term refers to the states and is a reminder of the fact that the country is made up of different states with their own qualities, the term "America" is more of a unifying term and perhaps more intimate. National identities are built at complex levels with many different stories that coexist to create the multiplicity of identities. For instance, the identity created by the label "Incredible!ndia" and the stories that make up that image could be very different from the label "India Inc." and the stories that make up an image of India as a financial player in the global scenario. While the story of India as told by the advertising campaign aims to bring more visitors to India, the story of India encapsulated in the "India Inc." term is meant to refer to the corporate structure of India and offer a clearer representation of how Indian economy is organized and how it contributes to the global economic system. Indeed, when, in June 2006, the American magazine *Time* used the term along with the picture of an Indian woman as its cover, a specific story was narrated about India to its audience.[10] Arguably, the identities created by the different terms and related narratives are indeed different from each other.

This multiplicity of narratives is a natural outcome of the complexity of everyday life. It is difficult to find a monolithic narrative that would completely encapsulate the identity of a person or a place. Very often, these different narratives offer the opportunity to create specific and contradictory narratives that serve different purposes at different times. Consider, for instance, the situation where an individual would say different stories about oneself—to those older and authoritative—the person could present a face that is of an obedient young man, whereas to friends he could come off as a rebellious youngster. These are two different identities that are presented through stories of behavior or utterances of attitude. The uniqueness of creation of multiple identities, as in this case, is the fact that these identities are produced by the individual for the individual because the person holds the power of "agency," where the individual could be the architect of one's identity because he or she is the agent or the storyteller, who produces and circulates the identity. In such situations, the multiple identities can be managed by an individual, and the person can also control behavior to match the identity narratives so that the stories, behaviors, and identities create a complete holistic picture. In some ways, the agent remains in control of the identities that are produced.

In the case of individuals, there is, however, another way in which identity narratives are produced and circulated. The alternative happens when others speak of an individual. These narratives could happen with the knowledge of the individual allowing the individual to retain a sense of agency on the narrative that is being produced. For example, I am often invited for talks at different academic conferences and forums. In such cases, the person introducing me to the audience would often ask how I want to be introduced. In that collaborative moment, a specific identity

---

[10] http://www.time.com/time/covers/0,16641,20060626,00.html

is produced about me by someone else, albeit with my approval and advice. The more insidious form of such identity production happens without the individual holding any sense of agency over the production. The identity is produced entirely by the other and in its worse form, this could be considered libel where a set of lies become the narrative that produces the identity. It happens in many different conditions ranging in the form of eulogies at funerals to hurtful remarks by an ex-partner. Such narratives could glorify a person just as such narratives can completely destroy the identity of an individual. In some cases, the individual would have no control on these narratives.

The lack of control can be attributed to the notion of power associated with the agency. When an agent has the power to speak, the person retains the power to shape one's identity narrative. When that power is nonexistent, then the narrative creation can be hijacked by those who have the power to speak. In the 1988 seminal essay called "Can the Subaltern Speak?" renowned Cornell University professor, Gayatri Spivak,[11] presented the argument that inequities of power can quickly silence a person or a group, and the only alternative of narrative creation then resides on those who are in power to produce the narrative for the other. In that process, the other is made a subject of a narrative and offered many different identity elements that could be very different from the "reality" of the subject that is being narrativized. Indeed, the work of Edward Said[12] and the arguments of *Orientalism* are also based on the fact that the European colonizers have had the advantage of providing their own unique and biased version of the "orient" that the colonizers encountered and then described in their words.

These narratives without agency are most often related to groups of people and to specific places as demonstrated in the works of Spivak,[13] who deals with people, and Said,[14] who deals with places. The narratives play the role of offering multiple identities

---

[11] G. Spivak, "Can the Subaltern Speak?" in *Marxism and the Interpretation of Culture*, eds. C. Nelson and L. Grossberg (Urbana-Champaign: University of Illinois Press, 1988).

[12] E. Said, *Orientalism* (New York: Vintage Books, 1978).

[13] Spivak, "Can the Subaltern Speak?"

[14] Said, *Orientalism*.

precisely from the perspective of the narrator and no longer from the perspective of the narratee. The worldview of the narrator then becomes the governing logic of the narrative, and whatever lens becomes the eyeglass of the narrator colors the narrative. It is the point of view of the narrator that determines the way the story is told. If a person likes another individual then that perspective would determine how a person is described. Many scholars would call this perspective the "ideological position" of the narrator. Here I use the term ideology in the way that Althusser[15] would have used it as a set of material practices that determine the worldview of a person. These material practices are simply what people do—what they eat, how they eat, how they dress, how they greet strangers— the list continues and in some ways, ideology and culture become similar terms since both could allude to practices. The strength of mobilizing the idea of ideology lies in the fact that ideologies struggle with each other and any moment, some ideologies become dominant where that dominance informs many different aspects of life including social, political, financial, and representational practices that make up everyday life. The struggle between ideologies happens at many different levels where the dominant ideology tries to retain the power over language and narration so that their version of "reality" becomes the conventional narrative allowing the powerful to obtain and retain power.

Consider, for example, the arrival of the early Europeans to the coasts of Africa. The visitors brought with them an ideology— material practices—which they considered to be appropriate and superior. When they encountered a different set of practices, the expected ideological struggle ensued, but the Europeans prevailed because they were able to use the specific languages and descriptors that became the natural and conventional way of describing the people and the practices that the Europeans encounter. We still live with that language as the word "native" is used to describe the people the Europeans encountered and the word was imbibed with all that is negative, savage, and inferior when viewed through the ideological lens of the visitors.

---

[15] Louis Althusser, *Philosophy of the Encounter: Later Writings, 1978–87* (New York: Verso, 2006).

It is important to note the relationship between narrative, power, ideology, and silence because nations and geographic spaces find themselves in a curious condition where there is no mechanism for the "nation" to gain agency by "speaking" for itself. A place is always and already spoken for. Yet, as Benedict Anderson has pointed out, communities and nations are imagined around the way they are spoken for and represented through languages and images. It is around specific utterances such as "Incredible!ndia" and "India Inc." that a nation and its people are imagined by the onlookers. Yet the country does not hold any agency on the way it is represented; but it only offers the material that would now be carefully constructed and then distributed to a global audience. It is, however, important to note the way in which such representations become critical in what kind of attributions are made to a place, country, and people.

ATTRIBUTIONS

I often ask my undergraduate students what they know of and think of specific places in the world. For instance, the very name of Egypt still conjures up in the mind the images of pyramids, desert, and Islamic people. Setting aside for a moment the source of these images, it is useful to follow through the attributions that people would make to a place and its people based on the way in which the place has been spoken for through numerous narratives. These attributions result in specific actions related to the place and its people. Attributions are not theoretical constructs, but these are real things that people do, based on their best understanding of a situation. These attributions might not be accurate, but they usually appear to be completely authentic to the persons making the attribution. Indeed, when a person truly believes that everyone in Egypt is a Muslim, there will be consequent ways of thinking of the people and eventually those attributions will show up in everyday interactions with the people of the place. Attributions offer a road map, albeit faulty, for behavior and most of the people rely on these to make decisions about behavior in everyday life. Lacking these signposts, there would be constant confusion about doing the "right" thing. Such confusion produces a sense of anxiety that could be debilitating and could eventually paralyze normal behavior of a human being.

The significance of attributions becomes especially mean-ingful when a person is placed in an unfamiliar cultural milieu. Consider a tourist in a foreign country; tour books tell a lot about a different place and people prepare for visiting the place by read-ing such books so that they have a narrative map of the place they would visit. It offers an identity for the place and that identity, in turn, offers the opportunity to create a set of attributes that would govern the behavior of the person when they visit the new place. If this line of reasoning was fully accurate, the knowledge based on the tour books, which represent the place and the people, would be all that one needs to be able to correctly make attributions, behave appropriately, and become a part of the culture of the place being visited. Yet, anyone who has stepped out of home to visit a differ-ent place would know that the reality of visiting new places brings in the notion of "culture shock." No amount of preparation, no amount of pouring over books, and no amount of browsing the Internet for information prepares one for the reality of what one encounters when actually in the place that has been represented in the images and languages that the visitor had access to. I see this every year; I bring a set of students from Wake Forest University to India for a summer study abroad class. I encourage them to read, view pictures, watch movies, and through the mediated informa-tion develop a sense of the identity of the place they would visit. Yet, the unique "smell" of India is something that they are not pre-pared for. As soon as they step outside the airport, they would ask the question "What is that smell?" It is a phenomenon for which they were unprepared, and, thus, they could not decide on their behavior related to smell since there was no prior knowledge and consequently no opportunity to prepare attributions.

CONSEQUENCES OF ATTRIBUTIONS

The most important consequence of the process of making attribu-tions is the way in which behavior is influenced by what one believes about the other. The authenticity of the knowledge becomes much less important than the way in which behavior is altered because of the attributions. There are many examples of this process and many have been on both ends of the attribution process. In some situations, one becomes the attributor where a specific behavior is demonstrated based on the information one has. Consider, for example, the simple notion of attributions related to language. Many years ago, my wife and I were at a Chinese restaurant in Winston-Salem, North Carolina. It was clear that the restaurant's owner was from China based simply on the looks of the person, and we were quite aware that we were in North America. It is well known that many immigrants from China have set up Chinese restaurants all over America, and the identity narrative associated with the owners revolved around attributions such as the fact that they were often the first generation of immigrants to the USA, did not have very good English language skills, were family-run businesses, and other such "known facts." My wife and I also operated under these normative assumptions of the identity of the owner and were talking about the restaurant and its lack of something I do not remember any more in Bengali to each other. Being from West Bengal, in India, Bengali is our "mother tongue," and we decided to use that language, attributing it to the fact that for a Chinese owner in North Carolina, it would be impossible to understand Bengali. The identity narrative simply would not allow that.

In about 10 minutes, Mr Lucas, now a dear friend of ours, walked over to our table and started a conversation in Bengali with us. My wife and I were simultaneously embarrassed and surprised. We, as attributors, had made a horrendous mistake in creating the identity narrative of the owner of the restaurant. Over the years, we became friends with the family, who had actually immigrated to USA from Calcutta, India. That family and our family grew up in the same city in India before coming to America. The fundamental identity narrative that led us to the attributions and our behavior was erroneous. To our defense, it could be argued that the chance of a person who looks Chinese and operates a restaurant in America knowing Bengali is very slim. In most of the cases, as attributors, we would have been correct since the normative identity narrative that we were working with is usually accurate making the behavior accurate as well. In other words, chances of such an event repeating itself would be slim, suggesting that behaving in a particular manner, based on attributions, is generally a norm in most of the societies, and except in rare cases, that behavior is accurate.

Similar things also happen when attributions are made toward a person and one becomes the target of the behavior because one seems to fit into a certain identity narrative. The incident takes on a different slant when considered from the perspective of Mr Lucas. From that point of view, the person faced an unfair, incorrect, and inauthentic pattern of behavior because of the fallacy of the attribution. It happens often. I remember that on an intercontinental flight from New York to New Delhi, the stewardess offered me a cup of coffee with sugar and cream added to it. When I declined it and asked for black coffee, the steward exclaimed, "But you are Indian and Indians don't drink black coffee." Again, a pattern of behavior based on normative attributions. Such consequences of attributions surround us constantly since representation-based attributions are the only things we can rely upon when we find ourselves in an unfamiliar territory and we are compelled to behave in a normative way.

This discussion about attributions, however, begs a commentary on the idea of "stereotype," which is a commonly used term in discussions of psychology and sociology. The literal meaning of the term, derived from the Greek words "stereos" and "typos," is "solid impression." It refers to an unchanging and permanent impression that can be reproduced and recirculated in a very convenient manner. Thus, the term was used to refer to the printing process for a long period, until American thinker and commentator, Walter Lippmann, used it to refer to human beings and impressions of human beings. In writing about the notion of stereotype, Lippmann was especially concerned about the way in which journalists would write about events, places, and people using preexisting images in their minds about what they were writing about. This idea was later developed into the theoretical area of stereotype analysis. The key to this analysis lies in two areas of emphasis (a) assumptions can lead to stereotypes and unfair judgments about individuals and groups and (b) stereotypes affect our lives. These two elements are similar to the discussion about attribution and behavior that I have presented here. Indeed, the attributions, in addition to being motivated by representations, are also often based on stereotypes where assumptions about a group lead to the attributions about specific members of the group. This leap, from assumptions about a group to assumptions about an individual who is expected to be a part of the group, is an important aspect of the way in which stereotype affect our lives. There has been much research in America, where race stereotypes are rampant, to show that personal awareness of existing stereotypes can affect personal behavior. For instance, it has been related to issues about academic performance and race stereotype where assumptions about the "expected" performance of children of specific races can affect the actual performance of the child. When a child, just based on the fact that the child looks Asian, is expected to be good in mathematics and science, then the child sometimes works harder to fulfill that stereotypical expectation. In this case, the assumptions, the identity narrative, the attributions, and the behavior line-up in a coherent whole, eventually strengthening and perpetuating the assumption.

What is, however, missing in the convenient alignment of assumptions and attributions is the urgency of examining the source of the assumptions. I make the argument that a portion of these assumptions are indeed based on the way in which the narratives are produced, circulated, and made to appear as the authentic and appropriate assumptions of the group. This is why it is important to examine the narratives as narrated by authors who might be a part of the group about which the narrative is produced and by authors who do not belong to the group. It is in the juxtapositioning of these narratives which the audience of the narratives eventually uses as the basis of their assumptions. It is important to note that it would be naive to claim that the assumptions are based entirely on the public narratives. There are many other interrelated factors that help to create the assumptions. For instance, one's religious upbringing could easily lead to assumptions about other religions. In the same manner, a few encounters with people of a particular racial group could lead to assumptions and attributions about everyone else of that group. However, I would argue that similar other sources of assumptions work in tandem with the publicly circulated narratives, and the eventual assumptions are products of the interconnection between these different factors that lead to the production of the assumptions.

NARRATIVES MATTER

As suggested here, it is commonplace for people to make assumptions and then act in specific ways because they rely on the "best possible" information that allows them to deal with a specific situation. In an ideal world, this best possible situation would indeed be complete and authentic information that a person has internalized and then acted in a way where the behavior is appropriate within a specific cultural circumstance. However, the best we have is actually a set of stories that are available to the people as they try to make judgments and assumptions. Therefore, a way to understand the patterns of behavior is to examine the stories that inform the behavior. Psychologists Martin Fishbein and Icek Ajzen suggested in 1975 that people go through a specific "reasoned action" when they behave in specific ways. Within their theory, they suggested that the reasoned action was motivated by the specific attitudes people held about issues, which, in turn, offered the rationale for action. In this model too, which has become the basis for much research on why people behave the way they do, there is an emphasis on attitude. The model, however, does not make much of the way in which attitudes are produced. Here too, the assumption is that attitudes are the result of environmental and other factors that determine how people think. I would submit that in the twenty-first century when we are surrounded by an abundance of messages, attitudes are indeed produced partially by the narratives we are exposed to.

There are many different ways in which the abundance of messages can be analyzed. Many scholars of mass media have offered many different ways of understanding the messages that surround us. Amongst the various theories, the ones that I use to offer my analysis are based on the overall presumption of Walter Fisher's narrative paradigm that I have discussed earlier. Within this theory, the authenticity of a story retreats to the background as long as the story appears to be true and believable. Fisher offers the notion of narrative coherence which deals with the internal logic of the story built up of a beginning, a climax, and a closure. Independent of whether the story is true or not, people would rely on a story that appears to be coherent in structure and thus make it believable. Similarly, Fisher[16] suggests that a story would appear to be authentic if it holds narrative fidelity. Here, the reference is to the extent to which a story matches the beliefs and experiences of the listener. If a story comes close to what the audience already believes in, then there is a greater degree of reliance on the worldview presented in the story. A story with coherence and fidelity thus becomes the basis of the assumptions and attitudes that govern behavior.

It is, therefore, necessary to be able to analyze stories to understand how they are constructed to create the narratively rational reality where the stories matter more than anything else because there is no other reality to access other than those produced through the carefully constructed narratives. In other words, for the average Indian, the "reality" of America is often produced through the stories about America. If indeed, the stories have been constructed in a manner that they are coherent and maintain fidelity then an "authentic" reality has been constructed about America for the Indian person. The key to this process is the way in which the story is constructed.

Since stories are indeed deliberately and carefully put together, it is possible to take apart the stories and understand the underlying logic of the construction and the intent of the author in constructing the story in the manner it is being presented. A French philosopher and author, Jacques Derrida, offered the argument that the deconstruction of a narrative offers a window into the underlying worldviews that motivate the rationale for producing and circulating a specific narrative. For instance, in old Soviet Russia, one could argue that every narrative served the purpose of maintaining a regime and the deconstruction of the narrative would have demonstrated how the stories helped to keep a system in places. The process of deconstruction relies on looking for specific traits in the narrative such as the narrative codes suggested by Roland Barthes[17] or by considering the specific narrative structure as theorized by Vladimir Propp. Along with them, some other

---

[16] Fisher, *Human Communication as Narration.*
[17] Roland Barthes, *The Pleasure of the Text* (New York: Hill and Wang, 1975).

theorists have offered ways of considering a narrative that allows for understanding the important role of narratives in contemporary society and the role of narratives in determining attitudes, assumptions, and behaviors.

In this book, the focus is on narratives about India. When I first dealt with this question in the early 1990s, the landscape of narratives about India, as available to the Western audience, was mostly composed of movies, occasional novels, and stories in the news. The scenario has changed significantly in the last three decades. Over the 30 years, there has been a global embracing of the digital modes of narrative production and distribution. It is no longer the case that an average American is exposed to in frequent movies about India. Indeed, in the closely connected digital world, many different narratives with many different authors and many different motives compete for attention in the public sphere. Unfortunately, these representations are often produced and circulated by "authors" with different ideologies and motivations. Specifically, in the twenty-first century, there has been an explosion in the opportunities to be an "author," producing more representations now than what existed even a couple of decades ago, for instance, the centrality of production and distribution of digital information. More people, groups, and institutions have found a voice now than ever before in the history of human civilizations. It is almost like the Biblical Babel that one is in now. It has been described in the Genesis that there was a place, which God ordained, where people will have their language "confounded" so that they do not comprehend each other and in that confusion, the blasphemous intentions of building a tower to Heaven would be automatically thwarted. It is a similar confusion that we face now where the multiplicity of agents and authors with their contradictory representations and consequent identity narratives offer the basis for making the attributions that become central to behavior. Behavior, both flawed and appropriate, is based precisely on the way in which representations are produced and circulated. In many ways, when asking me to return to India, the young women operating off a set of attributions they made of me. To some degree, their behavior was accurate since I had come from India and could potentially go back. However, had I been a "second generation"

Indian, such as my son born and brought up in America, the statement "go back to India" would have been meaningless, yet such as an attribution could be made simply on the basis of the narrative that his physical features produce.

An examination of the multitude of different narratives helps to arrive at a provisional conclusion about the way in which these different narratives offer an image of India and the people of Indian origin. The analysis is based on the theoretical principles discussed here and the methodology, which will be explicated in the later chapters, drawn upon the traditions of narrative and semiotic analysis. In the next chapter, I offer an overview of the significant changes that have happened in the last 30 years that lead to the reasons for reconsidering how India is being presented to the West.

2. INDIA AND INDIANS: CHANGING PLACES AND PEOPLE

In order to write about change, it is necessary to recapitulate the past. For my book of 1994, my goal was to discover how India and Indians were represented through the Western lens of cinema made in Hollywood and other parts of the West. With that goal in mind, I performed a close study of nearly 60 different movies that were made within a span of almost 60 years from the days before India gained independence from the British to the 1992 Roland Joffé movie, set in Calcutta, called the *City of Joy*. This range of movies was analyzed using the methods of textual and narrative analysis keeping the Western audience in mind and deconstructing the texts in a manner that an audience of non-Indians would do. This decision was predicated on the fact that the movies I looked at had the largest circulation in the West and made to appeal to the Western audience. The findings pointed to certain specific areas of representation that helped to create a cinematic image of India in the minds of the audience. I argued that this image of India and Indians had become the commonplace and ideologically acceptable image of the nation and its people. Indeed, the image was produced and distributed repetitively in Western movie theaters where the audience glimpsed India while sitting in the comfort of a "dream zone" produced in the Western multiplexes. Only a small number of viewers, such as me and my friends at the University of Illinois at Urbana-Champaign, cheered at the wide shots of the iconic Howrah Bridge of Calcutta in the Joffé movie; we also cringed at the depiction of monkey brain-eating religious despots in *Indiana Jones and the Temple of Doom*. However, to the majority of the audience, the movies created an un-contradictory and seamless image of India through the Western lens. It is useful to consider some of the key components of this image to position the focus of the current analysis.

INDIA THROUGH THE WESTERN LENS[1]

One of the key aspects of the representation had to do with the way in which the nation was depicted as a geographical entity. Every geographic space is branded with certain specific images that relate to the way the land looks and the iconic elements of the land. These are geographic narratives that have become commonplace in the world of images. Egypt conjures up images of sand dunes and deserts; America brings to the mind the Statue of Liberty and the Niagara Falls. In the analysis of the movies, the geographic image of India was that of the jungle—untamed and exotic. In parts, this jungle was dangerous with lethal predators, and in other parts, it was composed of unique and amazing traits from quintessentially Indian animals to geographic features that could only be found in India. The interesting aspect of this image was the fact that India has been presented as a metaphoric jungle where the urban spaces also become as much a jungle as the literal forests of India. For instance, my analysis discovered that films such as *City of Joy* painted the city as a jungle of human predators preying on the innocent poor villagers that migrate to Calcutta seeking a better life but ending up being rickshaw pullers in the concrete jungle of the metropolis with its gang leaders and their henchmen.

---

[1] Much of this summary is drawn from Chapter 5 of the earlier book (Ananda Mitra, *India through the Western Lens* [New Delhi, India: SAGE, 1994]).

The films also presented the other jungle as in the case of the playful place of Mowgli, the animated protagonist in *The Jungle Book* where the forest is literally a place with happy characters, such as Baloo, the bear, and the bungling snake, Kaa. India, thus, becomes this jungle which is also viewed from the perspective of the Western White protagonist who finds himself—most of the time it is a male protagonist—who must negotiate this jungle and find a way to tame it. Indeed, my analysis showed that there was a specific motivation to create a geographic space that was hostile and exotic because that offered the narrative opportunity for the Western hero to be a hero. For instance, in *Around the World in Eighty Days*, Phileas Fogg gets the opportunity to rescue the damsel from the "jungle" event of sati and bring a sense of order to the chaos that is the Indian jungle. Even though such a protagonist is absent in *Salaam Bombay*, the theme of the urban forest is continued by Mira Nair, albeit a filmmaker of Indian origin, making a movie for the Western audience. This geographic notion of India is also supplemented with specific images of the religious landscape of India that the movies produce, further, forging a specific image of India and its people in the minds of the Western audience.

The theme of exoticism is continued in the way religion and its practices have been seen through the Western lens. As my analysis pointed out, the key to the representation of religion was in exposing to the Western audience the deviance of religious practices of India from those that the Western audience would be accustomed to. Specific cinematic strategies were used to highlight this deviance. In some cases, the process was outright shocking as in the case of religious leaders who would readily do human sacrifices to appease exotic goddesses such as Kali. Here, the image was un-contradictory and presented the local religion as pure evil since the very notion of a female deity could be foreign to much of the Western audience, let alone a goddess who sports four hands, one of which holds a severed head. To be able to present this to the Western audience, there could be a marketing coup where the very depiction of these images would draw the audience cringing in their seats and awaiting the moment when the Western protagonist would "save" the natives from such harrowing religious practices and beliefs. However, the unusualness of the religious practices of India is also represented in the films where the narrative presentation might not have been meant to be shocking, but still maintained the distance between the Western religious practices and the Indian practices. In the analysis, I alluded to the way in which Hindu marriage rituals are presented as spectacles in Richard Attenborough's epic biography *Gandhi*. Here, the Father of the Nation explains to a Western observer—representing the entire audience of the movie—the implications of the specific steps of the marriage rituals. In that explanation, the process is differentiated from what the audience would consider to be marriage, and, in that cinematic moment, a specific image of Indian religion is created and circulated. In this image, the two aspects that remain important, although at different degrees of emphasis, are the facts that Indians practice a strange religion with completely unusual rituals and, at times, these rituals are so repugnant that the Western protagonist must act as the messiah whose responsibility is to save the natives from their own traditions.

Consequently, one of the other key findings from the earlier analysis is the way in which the very notion of tradition has been represented through the Western lens. It becomes clear through the analysis that India is a place that is doused in a sense of tradition, which goes back thousands of years. This "age" of India is often presented as a rationale for the religious practices of the people. It is also the case that tradition becomes a burden since the traditions are ancient and inappropriate for the modern times. In describing the sense of "modernity," the analysis also demonstrated that the sense of the new and enlightened was offered to India through the process of colonization where the Western intruders were able to offer the civilized and modern alternative to the traditions of India. Movies often offered this interplay between Indian traditions and Western modernity, presenting this juxtaposition as a crisis that the narratives had to resolve and offer a closure where one would trump the other. Thus, in *Mississippi Masala*, the traditional practices of the Indians in diaspora in a southern state of America are called into question when the immigrant Indian female protagonist had premarital sex with an African-American. The movie makes much of this conflict attempting to place one against the other, encouraging the audience to develop their judgment about the way in which the traditional Indian might think when faced with such a situation. Similar conflicts are presented elsewhere as shown in the analysis. For example, in the movie *Bhawani Junction*, that depicts the moment of the loss of the colony, there is the interplay among tradition, modernity, and colonialism as the sustainability of the modernization of India is called into question and the Anglo-Indians, the products of two hundred years of colonial rule, are faced with the choice of remaining in the "old" India or go to the "modern" home in Britain. In such cinematic moments, India and Indians appear to be caught in a crisis of tradition that must be negotiated as the Western audience would shake their heads seeing the condition of India and being reminded of the need to save the people and the place.

The analysis of films, thus, produced an emergent image where India appeared to be a place that faced a series of crisis, but also appeared to be a monolithic cultural entity steeped in tradition, exotic in location, and made up of everyday-lived practices that set it distinctly apart from the lived experiences of the audience. Furthermore, the image was relatively consistent across the various filmic representations. The pressures to stay true to a formula and produce an ideologically consistent image that would remain within the latitude of expectation of the audience led to a process of recurring "safe" themes that would not call into question the natural and conventional image of a place and its people. Also, in the 1990s, there were fewer modes of producing and circulating images for the Western audience. Films remained the primary way of doing this. Television, at least in America, was far more focused on local narratives, and there were infrequent allusions to India and its people. There was no Internet to offer additional options of producing images.

This brief summary of the findings from the 1994 research offers the benchmark with which the findings presented in this book must be compared. However, the comparison can only make sense when the findings of the current analysis can be placed within the context of 2013. Much has changed in 2013, and these changes become relevant when considering the way in which India is presented on the Western screen. Indeed, these changes are related to the creation and circulation of the current image. Of these changes, I am particularly interested in the ways the audience of the West has gained greater access to a variety of media where India is represented, as well as the way in which these varieties of media are consumed by an audience that is no longer only the "audience of the West," but also an audience of Indian origin who might be in the West. First, it is useful to consider the shifting access to media.

ACCESS TO MESSAGES

In 2013, the Pew Research Center, which tracks the penetration of the Internet in America, reported that nearly 80 percent of the American population has access to digital data at home through a high-speed connection to the Internet or through a smartphone that allows the user to connect to the Internet. I would argue that this is perhaps the most significant change in the global media landscape since the access to the Internet alters both—the amount of information that is potentially available to the audience and the variety of information that is available. It is also the case that when this access becomes available, the information is consumed in different ways. Consider, for instance, the fact that in 2012, *The New York Times* reported,

> Adoption of the tablet—which made its debut just two years ago with the launch of the original iPad—is now at 31% of the U.S. population that uses the Internet, equaling 74 million users. That's up from 12%, or 28 million users, in 2011.[2]

The combination of access to the Internet and the adoption of tools, such as the tablet computer, offer opportunities for content consumption that is no longer restricted to the movie theaters or the television sets. Within this media environment, the process of image creation through the circulation of discourses and storytelling is happening in different media spaces, and the number and variety of stories are growing constantly as new stories make their appearance and are propagated through multiple means. The audience can access stories and the resultant images at any time and in any format they want. Consider, for instance, the increase in

---

[2] Phyllis Furman, "Tablet's Popularity is through the Roof, Nearly One-third of U.S. Internet Users have one: Survey," *New York Daily News*, June 19, 2012. Available online at: http://www.nydailynews.com/2.1353/tablets-popularity-roof-one-third-u-s-internet-users-survey-article-1.1097990

digital distribution of movies for personal consumption on a digital device that could range from a desktop computer to a smartphone. In America, one of the popular outlets for obtaining digital copies of movies has been Netflix. Subscription to Netflix allows users to legally watch movies that are available in the Netflix library. In the April of 2013, there were nearly 28 million Americans who were subscribing to Netflix.[3] The interesting fact about Netflix is that the company not only makes available the movies and TV shows, but the subscribers can also obtain programs that can be loaded into smartphones and tablets where the movie can be watched wherever they want. The growth of Netflix and other such distributors, like Vudu, has transformed what narratives people are gaining access to.

This transformation to access to narratives has also been influenced by another tool of digital media—personal video production and distribution systems. The most notable example of this process is the ubiquitous YouTube in America. While YouTube is a global phenomenon where anyone with access to the Internet can place content on the YouTube system and that content can then be viewed by anyone with access to the Internet, in America, in 2013, YouTube reached more adults in the 18–34 years age range than any traditional cable network. It is especially important since this is the age group that is seeking the narratives in the alternative digital spaces and gaining access to a far more diverse set of messages than their predecessors did who grew up consuming the images available through the movies I had analyzed in 1994. Things, such as YouTube, which also belongs to the larger ecosystem often called "social media," are changing the notion of access to media by allowing more people to access more information more frequently and more easily than ever before.

This access is also happening in a world where more people are also constantly moving from place to place, and the fixity of people as geographic homogeneous blocks is increasingly called into question. One of the consequences of this movement is the shifts in the composition of the audience. For example, the filmmakers who were conjuring the images in *Around the World in Eighty Days* were making the movie for the matinee audiences

---

[3] http://online.wsj.com/article/SB10001424127887323735604578439140120610354.html

across America, but the makers of Bollywood movies now have to deal with a heterogeneous audience that did not even exist when some of the movies mentioned in my earlier book were made. Another consequence of the movement is the increased probability, especially in America, of people of different national and ethnic origins coming face-to-face with each other and both needing some basis that can be used to understand each other. The chances of the audience of Phileas Fogg's antics did not anticipate they would meet a person who has physical features like the evil priest of the movie outside the movie theater getting out of a late model Mercedes-Benz car having come to watch the Bollywood movie playing in the same multiplex in Greensboro. The combination of greater access to messages and migratory conditions both need to be considered before beginning to analyze the message about India and Indians that is available on the Western screen. Thus, I consider the general issues of migration and diaspora and then the specific conditions of the Indian diaspora in the West.

MIGRATION AND DIASPORA

Starting in the 1990s, there has been an increase in the process of moving from one place to another with the intention of staying in the new place for more than the time a normal sojourner or tourist does. Consider the example of the United States which has historically been the destination of people from all over the world. The American government issues a special permission to enter and work in the US for elongated periods of time where the visitor does not become a citizen of the US but has to integrate into the American culture to create a comfortable quality of life. A limited number of these permissions—called H1-B visas—are issued annually, and the data suggests that starting in 2004, all of the 65,000 visas are used every year. Indeed, in some years, as in 2008, all the 65,000 applications were received on the first day that the applications were made available. While the demand for H1-B visas has fluctuated with time and the status of the global economy, it is the case that these statistics point toward the fact that people are moving from one to place to another at a relatively rapid pace. This movement, although of a small number of people, comes with a set of consequences.

A good way to consider the consequences is to consider the notion of "diaspora." The term refers to a broad set of issues that are involved with the processes of voluntary and involuntary movements. In its early use, the notion of diaspora was referred to the process of involuntary movement where large groups of people would be forced to move from one place to another. Thus, the term described the plight of Jews who were constantly made to move from place to place without ever establishing a "homeland" until the creation of Israel when the permanently diasporic Jews were able to come to a place they would call home. For Jews, the diasporic condition begins as early as the time when the Egyptian Pharaohs drove the Jewish out of their land, leading to the legendary exodus of the Jews led by Moses who parts the Red Sea to escape from Egypt. The history of the Jewish people has been one of constant nomadicity with the compulsion to maintain the Jewish identity and culture in the face of the challenges brought forth by the diasporic condition. Given the connection between Judaism and the diasporic condition, much of the discussions about diaspora focuses on the ways in which diaspora creates conditions where the "original" and the "traditional" cultural practices are tested and challenged since the people of the place where the diasporic life could find the practices of the diasporic unnatural or unconventional.

Indeed, it is the strong desire to maintain those cultural practices that often drives the diasporic to create their own enclaves and carve out spaces in the foreign lands, where the original practices of the culture can be continued undisturbed and out of sight of the majority of the culture of the place of adoption. It led to the original Jewish ghettos in European cities. Consider, for instance, the early ghettoes of the 1500s in Venice. Indeed, the English word "ghetto" is borrowed from the Venetian word "ghetto" that means slag, a product of foundries, since the Jews were confined to an island in Venice where the slag from foundries was disposed of as well. Over time, the term "ghetto" has been used to refer to any place where people with certain commonalities have lived together and have created a specific cultural way of life that is different from the way of life of the people surrounding the ghetto, which also, often, represents the dominant culture of the place. The key to the process is the preservation of a specific way of life and the ability to stay together.

Image 2.1. Typical Religious Celebration in the Home of a Diasporic Indian in the USA

Courtesy: Author.

The need to preserve a way of life amidst the movement from a place of origin to a new place is a key tendency within the diasporic conditions. This desire is motivated by many factors amongst which I would suggest that an important one is the desire to find a safe place where one's identity can be preserved by remembering and cherishing the narrative of the place of origin, which helps to partially relieve the pressure associated with producing a new narrative for the place of adoption. In other words, I can be "who I used to be" at the Indian marketplace on Devon Avenue of Chicago, as opposed to being "who I have become" at the Woodfield Mall outside of Chicago. This preservation could take many forms—from elaborate ones such as religious ceremonies in homes to simple ones such as wearing a specific outfit such as a sari when visiting with other diasporic Indian friends. Eventually, the notions of movement, the need to find a place to stick together, and the need to preserve something that could be lost easily, all came under the general umbrella of the term "diaspora," creating the space to consider diaspora not only as a product of involuntary and forced movement, but also as a condition that people would have to manage when one chooses to voluntarily move from one place to another.

Further, the sense of nomadicity attached to the original use of the term, as the Jews moved from one place to another at regular intervals, could be reestablished because the voluntary movements of the twenty-first century are fundamentally nomadic in nature. People do not necessarily move from one place to another and stay there for the rest of their lives. On the other hand, people move many times and each time they experience the diasporic condition. Consider, for instance, the data provided by the Bureau of Labor Statistics in the United States which suggests that 91 percent of the people born between 1977 and 1997 in the United States will stay at a job for less than three years. Many of the job changes could be accompanied by a change of place, some within the country and some to foreign places.[4] This is not just an American tendency, as the visa numbers indicate, or news reports from different parts of the world point out; for instance, the *Times of India* reported in 2013 that for the young Indian professional, "four jobs in less than two years no longer raise eyebrows."[5]

Such tendencies along with movements related to seeking higher education, better careers, and escape from repressive cultural, social, political, or military forces have created a dynamic global environment where people are moving much more than others creating new contexts of message consumption and creation that did not exist in 1994. This is a very different context from the context within which the movies such as *Gunga Din* and even *City of Joy* were produced and consumed. I consider it an important element in my analysis and thus offer a brief description of the Indian diaspora to contextualize what comes later in the book.

INDIAN DIASPORA

Much has been written about the movement of people from the Indian subcontinent to many parts of the world. Authors such as Amitav Ghosh, Jhumpa Lahiri, Salman Rushdie, and many more

---

[4] http://www.forbes.com/sites/jeannemeister/2012/08/14/job-hopping-is-the-new-normal-for-millennials-three-ways-to-prevent-a-human-resource-nightmare/
[5] http://articles.timesofindia.indiatimes.com/2013-06-25/work/29765101_1_job-offer-job-satisfaction-job-hopping

have offered narratives and fictions that offer a human face to the process by which people of subcontinental origin now reside in nearly 100 countries across the globe. The story of the movement of people have been captured in academic volumes such as *The Encyclopedia of the Indian Diaspora*,[6] and in the creative work of people such as photographer Steve Raymer whose photographic documentation of Indians in diaspora shows that the "the sun never sets on this Diaspora a fact of geography."[7] A review of these various kinds of treatise on movement would show many of the different aspects of the diasporic condition, but within all of that, there is a common and underlying theme that plays an important role in defining the lives of people in diaspora—the creation of safe places in the country of adoption. The notion of place is especially important to reconsider given the ways in which new technologies have offered the creation of real and virtual places. It is also in these places that the messages are consumed. At certain points in the history of the diaspora, place for Indians have been defined by geographic locations, such as Edison, New Jersey, referred to earlier in the book and where I was told to return to India, or by Devon Avenue in Chicago where, even in the late 1980s, it was possible to rent the new release Hindi movies on videocassette. In such places, the people of the subcontinent found familiar practices, objects, and people. Walking in South Hall outside of London, one could encounter people sitting on *charpais*, eating *aalu parantha* and speaking in chaste Punjabi. Such were the public places where the people felt "safe."

Like others in diaspora, the diasporic Indian also constructed personal and private places where the inside of a house in America or England would be redesigned and appropriated to create a safe place, for instance, place of worship. Palatial homes of the financially successful diasporic could have entire spaces devoted to the place of worship—making the entire home "safe." Even the less financially fortunate would colonize a tiny section of a bedroom to create a safe place where Ganesh could be put for

---

[6] http://books.google.com/books/about/The_Encyclopedia_of_the_Indian_Diaspora.html?id=GvttAAAAMAAJ

[7] http://thetravelphotographer.blogspot.com/2007/09/steve-raymer-india-in-diaspora.html

daily worship and security of the home and its residents. These are the real spaces that the diasporic occupy and protect. In a similar vein, temples have mushroomed across America where the diasporic can worship communally in a safe environment and here, the practices of the community from the annual Garba dance to the naming ceremony of a child would all be safely conducted, in the place of adoption, but often out of sight of the others who dwell in the place of adoption. It is only with the maturity of the diasporic people and a better understanding of their own condition that there is a greater colonization of the "public" places of the country of adoption. Increasingly, "India festivals" have started to happen across the globe, where a public park, an auditorium, or a street block would be occupied and made "safe" as the diasporic celebrate their practices in full view of the others that make up the dwellers of the place of adoption. With time, the notions of real place and the way in which safety is conceptualized has shifted as the diasporic population has grown and matured. It is within these transformations of place outside India where the greater access to messages is also happening. Because of the greater visibility of people from the subcontinent, it is now the case that messages that represent India on the Western screen need to be aware of the ways in which the diasporic Indian has mobilized the public places of the West, making the Western audience different from the Western audience who consumed *Bhawani Junction*.

There is, however, another notion of space and place that becomes important to consider. The place is not necessarily only the real space that a person's body occupies, but new technologies, particularly those of the media, have offered opportunities to create discursive spaces where one can reside and feel the necessary sense of safety and gain access to the plethora of messages that are available on the Internet. I have argued elsewhere that the digital technologies allow individuals to "live" in a virtual place where they are surrounded by people like them. In the 1990s, this was possible through the Usenet groups, such as soc.culture.india, where the diasporic would be in the company of other Indians, as the name of the group would suggest, and discuss social and cultural issues related to India. The participation in the discussion, and thus the occupation of the place, was done through discourse and language where the dwellers would not have a "real" physical presence, but through their utterances online, they would create themselves and the place as the "safe" place where discussions about Indian society and culture was allowed and welcome. Yet this safe place could be reached without ever stepping outside of one's real place because the entry into this virtual space was through the computer screen.

This place is created on the screen through which the diasporic individual can connect with and interact with a whole new world composed of the elements of the place of origin. As long as the screen is accessible, one's physical location could become unimportant and less relevant. Consider the process where a person in the United States is able to connect to the Internet and watch a live game of cricket being played in India. Such conditions were made possible through the emergence and popularity of satellite and Internet technologies which demonstrated that it was quite possible to be "in India" while physically being located elsewhere. This congruence was the result of the need for safe places as an increasing number of people from India were travelling and staying in different places, and the increasing sophistication of technologies that made it possible to create the real and virtual safe places.

One of the consequences of the creation of real safe places in specific enclaves across the globe and the production of the screen-based safe places was the increasing availability of Indian practices across the world. An Indian in the West, for instance, was no longer disoriented from the lack of availability of Indian things. Indeed, if one were to consider the matter of Indian food in the West, it is not that difficult to obtain Indian food in most of the Western places. Similarly, it is not difficult to access Bollywood movies on innumerable websites which provide immediate access to media from India. If one were interested in the most recent television shows in India, these are made available through satellite television and similar technologies in most parts of the world.

These conditions of the twenty-first century with respect to the creation of different Indian spaces which are increasingly visible to the Western audience coincide with two other tendencies that are hallmarks of the twenty-first century. First, like many other people, Indians are much more mobile now than two decades ago. In 2013, there were more people from India who travel for short or long durations to the West than has been witnessed in the history of India. These people are not the ones in the diaspora, but they are sojourners who are in the West for a short period of time. It is, thus, not uncommon to see people of Indian origin all over the world as they work in many different places or they travel because of the increasing affluence of the middle-class Indian who is now able to holiday in different parts of the world. Indeed, Bollywood has played an indirect role boosting the phenomenon of Indian tourism across the globe. For instance, Switzerland attracts a large number of Indian tourists only because movies produced in Bollywood have successfully imaged Switzerland to the vast Indian audience. While it is somewhat amusing, and it is no surprise, that the only restaurant at the end of the funicular ride to the viewing point for Mount Jung Frau is an Indian restaurant called Bollywood. That juxtaposition of cultures is precisely the objective of this book where I seek to demonstrate how the images on the Western screen can normalize the "place"ment of a Bollywood restaurant at the top of an Alpine tourist destination in Switzerland.

In order to contextualize the relationship between the safe places for the diasporic and the access to messages in the twenty-first century, it is also important to note that just like many other people with multiple identities, there is also an increasing number of hyphenated Indians, such as the Indian-American, who either through birth or naturalization have complex identity narratives. These are the people who might have migrated from India to America or could be the second and third generation children and grandchildren of people emigrated from South Asia many years ago. These hyphenated Indians are people who look like any other South Asian, but consider the West to be their home. These people face the diasporic condition as much as the newly arriving Indians. These are our children who, because of the choices made by people like me who immigrated to America, now must face all the elements of the diasporic condition. Especially in America, this is a usual narrative because most people in America can claim that movement played an essential role in their being in America. Yet, these later generation immigrants of Indian origin still stand out in the public White places of the West where they too must bear the burdens of the representations that are produced and circulated through the greater access to messages that everyone has. For instance, these are the people, like my 20-year-old son, who populate the college campuses of America as Americans, but share in the identity politics of the other 19-year-old Indian who have just arrived from India to study in the same college campus of America. They look alike, but come from two different worlds and each seeks out a safe place in the new world they share.

As a result of these two conditions—mobility and hyphenation of identity—the world is exposed to more people of Indian origin. The West, thus, has greater opportunities and needs to make judgments about the people who look like Indians, and with the greater access to messages, it is convenient to turn to the way in which India is represented on the Western screen to make the attributions. These conditions lead to attributions being made more often, and it becomes important to understand what these attributions are based on. Very often, the attributor has little access to information before making the attributions. To most of the people making the attributions, the diasporic condition is unfathomable; to them, the notion of a hyphenated identity is of no consequence and to the attributor, the idea and need for a safe place is completely foreign. Yet they must judge and they need a yardstick to measure with. The availability of messages has made the yardstick far more accessible than what it was in the 1980s and 1990s. In 2013, the attributor feels that the video they saw on YouTube of a Bollywood item dance while having an Indian home-cooked meal at the home of an Indian family, whose son is a good friend of their daughter, is indeed a representation of what it means to be an Indian—the Chikni Chameli on YouTube.

The analysis presented in this book, thus, deals with the combination of conditions that are quite a bit different from the historical context of the movies about India produced in the West in the 1960s, 1970s, or even the 1990s. In 2013, the audience of the West was much more diverse, far more exposed to the people of Indian origin, and even made up of people of Indian origin. This audience has a greater access to messages than what was available even in the 1990s. The audience is also much more in touch with people of the Indian origin living in the West, requiring the audience to be more aware of histories and attributes of people of the

Indian origin. Again, the messages on the Western screen offer guideline to make those attributions. The current analysis, thus, needs to be understood within the contexts of creating safe places for the diasporic Indian who constantly mingles within the West and carries the burden of the representation of Indians on the Western screen.

In the next chapter, I offer a detailed understanding of the term "screen" and its technological and cultural implications in the context of the creation of images of people of the Indian origin.

3. LOOKING AT THE SCREEN

Although the word "screen" has been around for a long period of time, there are few unifying definitions of what the word specifically means. The term is used in many different contexts, and within each context, it takes on its own meaning. Some of those meanings and descriptions are of little direct interest to the discussion here. However, it is important to review a few of those uses because I would be utilizing the metaphorical meanings of the word "screen" later in the book. To some, the term "screen" refers to a physical object that stands between the individual and an outside world. Thus, a "screen door" offers protection from the insects of the outside world while allowing the one inside to be able to look at the outside world without being troubled by some of the irritations of the outside. In America, many homes would boast of a screen porch, which is a space that is surrounded by metal or plastic mesh that keeps out the bugs but allows the dweller to be in touch with the outside. These physical screens act as filters, where some elements of the harsh reality of the summer evenings infested by mosquitoes in North Carolina, where I live, are kept out so that I can sit on my screen porch protected from the outside.

The notions of protection and filtering are important real life issues that we seek in many aspects of our everyday lives. We have a need to create safe places where one can get a sense of comfort and happiness that remains undisturbed by forces that we are troubled by. Earlier, we discussed the creation of immigrant enclaves and spaces where the diasporic is surrounded by the similar others, thus, "screening" out the rest. An invisible screen is created around these spaces which are often universally acknowledged indicators of turf where some are welcome inside the "screened" area while others are expected to stay out. The Jewish ghettos of Venice and the Indian Bazaars of Chicago have become the means of screening out and protecting spaces much like the screened porch offers respite from the elements.

The physical notion of the screen, as in the case of the screened door or the screened window, is also a filter through which the rest of the world can be experienced. Returning to the example of the screened porch in my house in North Carolina, many friends have mentioned that before we added the screened porch as an extension to our home, we used to sit on the open porch, bitten by mosquitos, but could look up and see the stars of the clear summer nights of the Carolinas and feel a sense of openness that has now been lost with the screen, the high ceiling, and the ceiling fan. In some ways, we have lost the freedom that the open porch allowed. Now things are filtered through the screen and some things, like the stars above, have completely been shut out. Screens are indeed filters. The clarity of the screen—whether it has become opaque because of the grime or whether it is clean and transparent—determines what we can see through it. In a famous scene from the 1992 Hollywood comedy *My Cousin Vinnie*, Joe Pesci, playing the role of the brash New York City lawyer, deposes a rural witness by pointing out that the screens on the window of the witness' house is so dirty that it would have impossible for the witness to make a positive identification of the suspects. When screens are dirty, there is always a chance of losing connection with the world that surrounds us. These two particular aspects of the screen—the fact it protects and it filters—becomes crucial in understanding the way in which screens operate. My interest is in the screens that become conduits to discourses and narratives. These are a different kind of screens, which are surfaces onto which narratives are displayed and protected once the narratives have been filtered through the creative work of the narrator.

THE SCREEN AS SURFACE

Once walking inside a pyramid in Egypt, the guide pointed toward the heliographics and the drawings on the walls inside a sanctuary within the pyramid and explained to us the meaning of the specific shapes and drawings. Similarly, looking up in awe at the ceiling of the Sistine Chapel in the Vatican City in Italy, I could not but marvel at the sheer narrative power and breadth of the work of Michelangelo as the surface of the ceiling was transformed, over a period between 1508 and 1512, into a "screen" that tells a story which is central to the Christian faith. When considered as a surface, the screen has been around for a long time. Consider for instance the paintings in the rock shelters of Bhimbetka. Located about 35 miles southeast of Bhopal, in India, the paintings on these rock surfaces have been dated to be as old as 100,000 years—which marked as indicators of the first human civilization in the Indian peninsula.[1] Cave paintings have been discovered in many other parts of the world, and scholars have examined these very carefully to get a sense of what the paintings represented and the narratives that were being presented through these works of art. Some of the research suggests that the paintings, for instance, those in the states of Tennessee and Kentucky in America, depict not only a way of life but also a way of thinking of the communities that did the paintings.[2] Eventually, the surface of the cave gave way to more sophisticated surfaces that morphed into the ubiquitous canvas of the artists all over the world.

Walking through the Uffizi in Florence or the Prado in Madrid, I have been enthralled by the massive canvasses that became the site of Renaissance artists who depicted complicated stories in their skillful use of the canvas surface and oil paint.

---

[1] http://asi.nic.in/asi_monu_whs_rockart_bhimbetka.asp
[2] http://antiquity.ac.uk/an fisket/087/ant0870430.htm

Paintings such as the "Surrender at Breda" completed by Diego Velázquez in 1635 or a more contemporary work of Georges Seurat at the Art Institute of Chicago called "A Sunday on La Grande Jatte," are some of the numerous examples of screens where a specific surface becomes the site of a narrative. These are narratives that capture a specific moment in time, making that the pivotal aspect of a narrative. These narratives remain embedded in cultural memory and some become the unquestioned representations of moments in history. These are the screens that filter reality for us, especially if these screens remain the only undisputed record of the moment. Standing in the refectory of the Convent of Santa Maria delle Grazie in Milan, I and the other visitors could not imagine any other representation of the last supper of the Christ— permanently etched in memory by the work of Leonardo da Vinci that was started in the last days of the fifteenth century. Screens like this provided the filtered and well-contained records that remain unchanged and static and often unquestioned. For the people of those days, these were some of the primary sources of narratives as they would look at the frescoes and wall paintings that depict the lives of people and gods. These were the beginning of the narrative screens on whose surface we continue to tell our stories.

The paintings in the caves of Ajanta, the canvasses that adorn the art museums across the world, and the murals that decorate the temples and churches have one important thing in common—they usually remain unchanged. It is unlikely that the ceiling of the Sistine Chapel or the painting of Madonna would be periodically changed. Indeed, much effort is spent in restoring some of the decay in these works of art to recover the original grandeur of these masterpieces and preserve them for the future viewers. For most artists, the white canvas is the place where the story will be told, and much care goes into the way in which the story is being told. Being married to an artist, I have watched my wife spend many hours imagining the way in which she would depict a scene on the white canvas, and there is always a moment of completion of the narrative. That is the moment when the painting is done, framed, and displayed on our living room wall. There are no further changes to the work—the white canvas has disappeared for ever. On the other hand, there has also been an interest in some artistic quarters to use the screen to project different works of art at a different time, and, in between, the white screen remains waiting for its next narrative.

Such "open-ended" screens, where different stories would be displayed at different times, have many origins, but a good example of such a screen is the white sheet used in the ancient art of shadow play. During the tenth century AD, under the regime of the Five Dynasties of China, the art form of shadow play was a popular form of entertainment to tell narratives related to Buddhism and ways of life in China.[3] Shadow play was created by skilled puppeteers who would use puppets that cast a shadow on a screen and the movements of the puppets told a story. The screen, in this case, was a white piece of cloth and was illuminated from the back so that the puppeteer could cast shadows from behind the screen. The screen was never touched with anything other than the light and shadow, and once the show was over, the screen was ready for the next show. Here, too, the screen offered the space to tell a narrative that was "filtered" by the puppeteers, and the screen was also the barrier between the narrative and the audience where the audience could "safely" witness grand narratives of battle and heroism told by skilled puppeteers. Much like the window screen or the large canvases of the museums depicting the artist's view of battles, these screens of shadow play also served the roles of offering a safe space for witnessing the filtered real world that remained beyond the screen. However, the screens of shadow play did not serve as permanent records of the narratives that were displayed on the screen, and these screens could be used repeatedly to tell different narratives.

This open-ended potential of the white screen, where light and shadow would tell different narratives at different times, captured the imagination of the audiences across the globe most remarkably with the invention of the Lumiere brothers in the late 1800s, when they demonstrated that moving pictures could be displayed on a white screen. Their invention was capitalized by the movie industries of the world, starting with America, and movie screen came into being as a site where filtered narratives could be displayed in the safety of the movie theater.

---

[3] http://traditions.cultural-china.com/en/17T21T13117.html

With the development and the growing popularity of films, the term "screen" became synonymous with movie screen and other terms were derived, such as "screening" and "screenplay," that all focused on the way in which the movie screen became the best-known screen in the popular culture. In the heydays of cinema in America, there was much emphasis placed on the way the screen was manufactured and improved upon. The grand cinema halls across the globe would be adorned with different types of screens, and as the technology of filmmaking developed, new forms of screens came into play. The invention of cinemascope and large film stock allowed for huge screens, and over the years, with the development of IMAX theaters, massive movie screens were installed in the best movie theaters in the world. Indeed, the largest known movie screen—the screen at Sydney's IMAX[4]—boasts of a height of 29.7 meters, nearly the size of an eight-storied building. All the movie screens, from the portable, quickly rigged screens for village screening of movies in rural India to the grandest theaters of the major metropolises of the world, had several things in common.

It was a screen that was fixed in one place. Just like one would have to go to a museum to see a work of art, the movie screen beckoned people to come to the movie hall to view the narratives unfold on the giant screen. The process required the creation of a dream-like setting, where the audience would be immersed in a peculiar condition and the people in the audience would experience the narrative within the boundaries of the screen. It is no surprise that psychoanalytic scholars, such as Christian Metz and Laura Mulvey, have used theories related to dream, as developed by Jacques Lacan, to discuss the ways movies influence the audience through the specific conditions under which the screen is used to narrate a story. Even now, the movie experience is one that has remained fundamentally unchanged from the early days of the movie screen—one goes to the cinema, sometimes as a social activity, and the narrative is filtered through the eyes of the filmmaker offering a safe site where extraordinary narratives can be enjoyed in the comfort of the modern multiplex.

---

[4] http://www.news.com.au/technology/worlds-biggest-movie-screen-that-is-297m-high-and-357m-wide-lifted-into-position-at-sydney-imax-theatre/story-e6frfro0-1226267360235

A major shift in the notion of the screen that offered an alternative to the movie screen happened with the development of Cathode Ray Tubes (CRT) that allowed for an electronic process to create images on a specially coated slab of glass. The CRT was first developed at the end of the nineteenth century, and, in 1907, Russian scientist Boris Rosing demonstrated that simple images could be displayed on the CRT making way for the television (TV) that was then commercialized in America as an alternative to the movie screen. Indeed, when TV became especially popular in America, during the golden age of TV (1940 to 1960), it came as a threat to the film industry because the TV screen now became a noticeable alternative to the movie screen offering narratives in a way that film simply could not by transforming the way in which the TV screen would relate to its audience.

The most important transformation of the screen was that it was released from the institutional spaces. Unlike the cave paintings that remained in the caves, the great works of art that remained ensconced in the museums of the world, and the grand narratives that were displayed in the movies theaters, the TV screen allowed for the narratives to enter the domestic space. The TV screen came inside the home of the watcher. In its early days in America, the TV equipment was called the "electronic hearth," a place where the family would gather to be entertained.[5] In other parts of the world, as TV became popular, it even became a sacred screen that would be worshipped because it brought home the classic texts of one's religion. Those who remember the phenomenon of TV series *Mahabharat* on Indian TV, in the 1980s, would recall the way in which the entire population of a nation would come to a standstill when the TV serials based on the religious epics would be broadcast.[6] The technology of the TV screen and the way it was used by the audience also began to reshape the notion of the screen transforming the meaning of the screen by focusing on the private viewing as well as the portability of the screen.

The proliferation of TV across the globe led to a condition in some parts of the world where the notion of the electronic

---

[5] Cecilia Tichi, *Electronic Hearth: Creating an American Television Culture* (New York: Oxford University Press, 1991).

[6] Ananda Mitra, *Television and Popular Culture in India* (New Delhi, India: SAGE, 1993).

hearth was quickly replaced by a much more personalized use of the screen. The notion of the hearth was motivated by the fact that many households, from the early days of TV to the 1970s, had only one TV at home. For instance, when TV was first introduced in Calcutta, India, on August 9, 1975, most families could only afford a single TV set that was placed in the "drawing room," as the public room is called in India, and everyone, including the domestic help and less affluent neighbors, would gather in that space to view the weekly music programs such as *Chitrahar* (film music) or the cricket matches. It was not unlike the situation in America in the 1950s when families would gather around the TV to watch shows such as *I Love Lucy*, first aired in 1951, and others. These were family events and a public consumption of the narrative. The situation, at least, in countries such as America, changed in two decades. By 1975, in America, nearly 43 percent of households reported owning two or more TV sets when the household was made up of an average of 2.88 persons. There was an increasing equalization of the number of people and number of TVs. In another 30 years, by 2006, it was reported that an average American household had more TV sets than people in the house.[7] The notion of public viewing of the TV screen was quickly being replaced by private viewing of the screen.

The proliferation in the number of TV sets was also accompanied across the globe with the development of alternatives to broadcast TV with a limited number of programs those were geographically restricted. In the early days of TV in India, the only program on the screen was offered by Doordarshan—the state-run noncommercial TV system in India. In other places such as United Kingdom, the TV stations offered by British Broadcasting Corporation (BBC) were the only options; in totalitarian systems such as old Russia, the only option was state TV offered by the Communist Party, and in commercialized systems such as America, the options were restricted to three national networks with their local affiliates. This led to a paucity of choice and single TV set was sufficient, and everyone watched what was available on the limited number of channels. However, the emergence of satellite and cable

---

[7] http://mjperry.blogspot.com/2010/05/more-tv-sets-than-people-per-household.html

distribution altered the landscape as more options appeared on the screen. Thus, there was a need for more screens as different people would watch different programs on their personal screens. The TV moved out of the "drawing room" and the living room and entered the bedrooms and the more private spaces. For the affluent, across the world, TVs were placed in every room—from the child's room to the parent's bedroom. People retreated to these spaces as the parents would watch the racier mini-series and the children would be restricted—often with the parent's locking out channels—to the age appropriate offerings. What had started as the communal screen that brought the filtered narratives offering to the safe space to consume the narratives, as a community gave way to narratives being consumed in the privacy of an individualized consumption experience. Different people were now watching the world through different filters that screened reality for them. The matter was further complicated when the TV screen became portable and new technologies allowed for time shifting the content consumption.

Screens, such as the movie screen or the larger TV sets, that adorned the living rooms and later every room of a home was supplemented by other tools that allowed the viewer to be able to move with the screen and consume the content at any place the viewer chose. While different companies experimented with the emergent Liquid Crystal Display (LCD) screens in the 1970s and 1980s, the first commercially popular portable TV was the Watchman brand released by Sony Corporation in 1982. This tiny device with a tiny screen became a popular gadget and people would now be able to carry the TV with them and watch shows anywhere they could pick up a broadcast signal. While this was a technological breakthrough, it allowed for the screen to become peculiarly private. The communal screen of the movie theater and the living room TV was now being replaced by a screen that allowed for complete private consumption. This privacy is important to note since this would become a part of the way in which screens would be used in the years following the 1980s, which was also the time when the computer technology was beginning to introduce yet another screen in the lives of consumers. The development of portability opened up questions of customized programming since people were watching TV on their own and there was an inherent desire to consume what the individual wanted and not what everybody else was watching. The technology of the 1980s did not allow personalization in terms of the content, but the Video Cassette Recorder (VCR) technology allowed the same with a choice of when TV programs could be watched.

The VCR was touted as a product that allowed users to watch their own preferred programming on the TV screen in the privacy of their own personal spaces at any time the person wanted to. It is, thus, not surprising that the screen and VCR combination became especially popular for a unique kind of programming—pornography. In the mid-1980s, the neighborhood video rental store in American cities would have a back room, behind a curtain, which would be stocked with pornographic video cassettes that the user could rent, take home, and watch in the privacy of their personal screen. The "blue movie" theaters that were located in the back alleys of downtowns of cities would soon go out of business because the patrons who consumed pornography, with many others, in the darkness of a movie theater on the movie screen were now renting the videos to consume the content on a different screen. This shift is significant because it demonstrated that some contents were more suitable for one screen as opposed to another. What pornography demonstrated is indeed the way in which the TV screen and the VCR filtered the world to the viewer and offered the "safe place" to consume content that could be considered inappropriate in the public space. In doing so, the screen further confirmed its metaphorical filtering and protecting role for the individual. This progression of the way in which the screen operates was supplement by the second appeal of the VCR—shifting the time when content would be consumed on the screen.

The VCR offered the opportunity to record a show that was broadcast at a certain time, often inconvenient to the viewer, and watch the content at a time more convenient for the viewer. At that time, the screen became a customized, filtered, and safe space where content could be consumed by the individual or a small group of individuals, without any concern about who else was consuming the content. Some VCRs offered the opportunity to skip over the advertisements further filtering the content and making the screen even more customized.

TV and VCR technology transformed the role of the screen, making it more of a filtering device that would create the safe space to consume personalized content. However, the development of the computer technology offered yet another screen to the individual—the CRT computer monitor. This was another inflection point when a new screen was introduced, bringing new content to the consumer.

The display technology of the computer screen was not much different from the ones used for the traditional TVs and later the flat-screen TVs. Indeed, these were essentially interchangeable technological systems. That tradition has carried on as TV became more LCD based and computer screens also followed the same path with displays that were slim and occupied lesser space. Eventually, with the development of the portable computer technology of laptop computers, the screen became a part of the computer and developed the portability that TV too had developed. While the technology of the computer screen display was similar to TV, the computer screen added a component to the notion of the screen that was absent in all of the other screens previously—the notion of interaction with the screen. This was a completely new element to the filtering aspect of the screen. Consider, for instance, how a visitor to an art museum is constantly reminded that one must not touch the artifacts. A person is expected to watch from a distance and there was no mechanism for the person to truly interact with the art displayed on the canvas. Indeed, the defacing of art could be considered a social and criminal offense and could draw global condemnation. Later, with the movie screen as well, the notion of interaction with what was on the screen was impossible and one could only watch as a passive viewer.[8] In some odd cases, the audience would find ways of interacting with the content of the screen in unconventional ways. For instance, a provocative cabaret dance in an Indian movie theater could lead to people throwing money at the screen or people would dress up as characters of the cult classic, *The Rocky Horror Picture Show*, and

---

[8] There is a large body of scholarship in mass communication research that makes much of the way in which the "audience" of mass media such as cinema has been considered a passive audience with little opportunities for interaction with the programming.

enact scenes from the movie in front of the screen while the movie would have its screening on Halloween night in many movie theaters in America.[9,10] These were bold attempts at interactions that continued with the TV screen where people would attempt to interact with the program hoping for a "two-way communication" between the program and the audience. However, the interaction was not a part of the way in which the screens and the content distribution technology was established. It changed with the arrival of the computer screen because it had arrived with another piece of essential computer technology—the keyboard—which acted as the extension of the human hand and allowed the user to interact with the tool before him. Now, with the keyboard, the users could use their hands to produce logical commands that appeared on the screen as they were typed, and the display on the screen could be manipulated based on the commands that were provided. Now the user of the technology was the one creating the filters and the safe space that the screen represented.

Interactivity had been a goal of TV for a long period of time when there were experiments such as "pay per view" and "on demand" programs would be offered by cable and satellite operators so that the viewer could choose what to watch on the screen. These services were limited in scope and allowed for simple manipulations, such as pausing the program or rewinding to the beginning of a show. The interactivity did not allow for a two-way communication between the screen and the user where the user could actually see immediate responses to commands delivered by the combination of the keyboard and the screen that the computer offered. With the growth of computing technology and increasing the reach of connectivity to the Internet and the

---

[9] Ashish Rajadhyaksha talks about the way in which the audience identifies with what is happening on the screen by actions such as throwing money at the screen or going into a trance during devotional songs. (see, Ashish Rajadhyaksha, "The 'Bollywoodization' of the Indian Cinema: Cultural Nationalism in a Global Arena," *Inter-Asia Cultural Studies* 4, no. 1 (2003): 25–39, http://isites.harvard.edu/fs/docs/icb.topic1218620.files/All%20Readings/rajadhyaksha.pdf)

[10] For the history of the way in which the audience participation began with *The Rocky Horror Picture Show*. See, http://www.rockyhorror.com/history/howapbegan.php, where the author discusses how there are elaborate propos and scripts that the audience use to interact with the screening of the movie.

popularity of programs such as World Wide Web (Web), the user could now create personalized narrative spaces where the stories that the screen filtered for the user were partly decided by the user. Examples of such operations could be traced in the development of the customized news delivery systems where users could now decide exactly what news the screen would display. For instance, when I am interested in news, I would focus on the news of my hometown—Winston Salem—as well as news from Calcutta where my relatives live and news from Philadelphia where my son goes to college. The personalization that the individual TV screens offered with the abundance of screens at home was further focused with the interactivity produced narratives that the computer screen brought forth. Each person with the computer screen could now create a personal safe place that, much like the screened porch, kept out the unwanted elements—narratives—and allowed in only what the user preferred.

This increased customization of the screen had the potential of how narratives would be produced and consumed. With the interactivity came the capability for institutions to know exactly what the user wanted to consume and institutions, such as advertisers, found the opportunity to provide exactly what the user wanted. The consumer was satisfied that no "unwanted" and "unnecessary" information was streaming in through the computer screen. The notion of creating the safe narrative and discursive space was further sharpened by the fact that the interactivity allowed users to create their own narratives and stories that could be displayed on their screen. The screen became a representation of the real person who was interacting with the screen. The growth of different systems called social media programs, best characterized by Facebook, offered the opportunity to look at the computer screen and see the self-reflected back where the self was a careful construction and the representation of the real person who was interacting with the screen. In many ways, the interactive computer screen came "alive" that no other screen had ever done before. While the movie screen remained completely static and the TV screen offered limited opportunities for interaction, the computer screen became the digitally screened porch where the user could create his/her own space and invite his/her chosen narratives and discursive representations of the people he/she wanted to interact with. As Facebook declared in their campaigns, Facebook profile became the space where the individual resided on the screen and interacted with "friends" who appeared as status updates on the computer screen.

Even though the computer screen offered some unique opportunities, the user still had to deal with at least two screens at home—TV and computer. It changed with yet another development in the technology where the narratives delivered on different screens coalesced into a single screen. This process is often called convergence.

The notion of convergence arises from a world of tools where engineers felt that there was an advantage in carrying a single tool to serve many different functions. One of the best-known convergent tools is the legendary Swiss Army Knife. It was built in the late 1800s when there was a need for the officers of the Swiss Army to have a knife that could do multiple tasks, such as opening a can or disassembling the Schmidt–Rubin M1889 service rifle of the army. Over the time, "knife" has been morphed into a tool that could include a data storage device for digital data as well as scissors. However, the notion of convergence is best demonstrated by a tool like the legendary knife when a single tool would offer different functions.

It happened in the realm of the screen as well with the rapid availability and adoption of digital tools that included the traditional computer, digital TV, ever larger smartphones, and different kinds of digital delivery of narrative content that could be consumed on a converged screen. For instance, with the availability of tools such as Apple TV, Roku, and Google TV, it is possible, in many parts of the world, to use a TV to browse through web pages. At the same time, using a large monitor connected to a home computer, it is possible to watch movies using companies that offer streaming digital files of popular movies. On the other hand, using the large screen of a smartphone and services that offer digitized TV shows, it is possible to watch a recent TV episode, from anywhere in the world, on the screen of the personal smartphone. It is the new screen that has become the site of the narratives. Many narratives converge on this screen and other traditional screens, like the movie screen in the theater, has responded to it with digital enhancements such as large screen formats, 3D projections, and better seating and other comforts in the theater. The traditional TV screen has responded to the convergence with larger screen sizes and greater interactivity by converging the internet-based resources with the traditional fare of TV. The computer screen has offered the seduction of interactivity by letting users do many tasks simultaneously on the same screen, and finally, the smartphones and tablet screens have offered privacy and portability along with what the computer screen offers.

The term "screen," as seen in this discussion, is a multifaceted work referring to many different things and concepts. In a way, a screen works in "real life," offers protection and filters out the undesirable components of life, such as mosquitoes on a summer night. Once the screen is considered as a surface where a narrative unfolds, the screen continues to filter and protect—showing only the desirable elements of the narrative, keeping out the disturbing elements of a narrative. As the screen has transformed from the static of a painting in a cave to the dynamism of the blank screen of Chinese shadow theater, so has the way in which the narratives have been told and consumed. Later, as the blank screen becomes the site of many narratives, told by the grand masters of storytelling, such as Warner Brothers of Hollywood and Yash Chopra of Bollywood, have enthralled the reader with the superbly filtered narratives, which in the language of film is called "editing." The idea of the screen was again called into question with the availability of the narratives at home—through the TV screen—as sites where the family could gather and enjoy the tales told by the storytellers who brought the machinations of the everyday life to the screen. Perhaps, the greatest transformation of the screen happened when the computer filtered the world for the user through the "Windows" of the computer screen, as Bill Gates offered the aptly name portal to the world. It is through the screens on the laptop, digital TV, smartphone, and handheld gaming systems that we experience the world today.

It is, thus, a peculiarly unique technological moment we inhabit today. There are ongoing experiments with "wearable technology," such as the glasses produced by Google which will bring the converged screen right before one's eyes and the real world, when witnessed through these glasses, would be filtered and augmented by the interactive information brought to the front

Image 3.1. Different Screens that Surround Us

Courtesy: Author.

by the glass. In a more cyborgian future, the screen might even be embedded into our biological body making us the true man–machine combination—the cyborg. I would suggest that, within the boundaries of media, the screen is no longer the movie screen or the TV screen, but the screen is made up of a set of different screens which could converge on a single device but bring forth different narratives with different levels of authorship of the narratives depending on the screen one is using at any moment.

Therefore, it is important to seek the many different ways in which a culture is imaged and imagined on the various screens to see what the differences are between the screens, and eventually, see if indeed a universalized image of a culture emerges from the combination of the screens where the culture is narrated. In the rest of this book, I examine the notion of India and Indians on several different screens to discover the key elements of the images and then consider what "India" one would encounter depending on the screen one uses as the filter. It is way different from the 1980s when I was motivated to discover India on the movie screens of Hollywood. Now, in the beginning of the twenty-first century, a different India emerges as many screens compete for attention presenting many different images of the nation and its people. I begin with the traditional and trusted movie screen.

4. THE MOVIE SCREEN

The Western screen that has spent the most narrative time with India is the movie screen. It is the popularity of India on the movie screen that motivated the 1994 book, *India through the Western Lens*, and the accompanying research that included numerous movies starting with the ones made in the 1940s and 1950s, and leading up to the late 1990s. As indicated in the previous chapter, the analysis demonstrated three major points: (a) the Western lens produced an image that attempted to "produce a geographical space that is simultaneously splendid in appearance and hostile in nature."[1] The focus on space was particularly important since the space was alien and foreign to the audience. (b) The issue of religion in India by projecting an image of "exotic and strange religions with violent and malevolent gods and goddesses who require deviant rituals."[2] It worked well to produce a comfort zone

---

[1] Ananda Mitra, *India through the Western Lens* (New Delhi, India: SAGE, 1994), 177.
[2] Ibid.

for the Western audience knowing that they were ensconced in a safe religious space, and the most they had to deal with was the deviance of the malevolent priest in *Indiana Jones and the Temple of Doom* who would feast on raw monkey brains blessed by his deity. (c) The image of a place with "long history and antiquity"[3] which was modernized and saved by the colonialists who civilized the place. The final image that was produced could be analyzed using these four major vectors—place, religion, antiquity, and colonization—offering an insight into the way in which India would appear to the audience who would look at India through the Western lens. In this chapter, I argue that the current image produced on the Western movie screen is built around a different set of factors. The shift might not necessarily indicate a shift in the dominant ideological way in which the region and its people are represented for the Western audience, but it could indicate that new representational strategies are being mobilized to create a specific image that has to enter into a narrative and representational struggle with the other screens that are at play in 2014.

WHAT TO LOOK AT AND HOW TO LOOK

The discipline of film analysis is vast and encompasses a multitude of analytical methods that span from the aesthetic analysis of film to psychoanalytic look at films to discover the way in which a film can become appealing and impactful. The use of any one of the specific analytic lenses is predicated by the specific questions that the analyst seeks to answer. Those who are writing a popular treatise about a movie to be published in the popular press could well adopt an aesthetic stance, whereas a professor interested in uncovering the way in which films re-describe the woman as an object of desire for the male viewer could adopt a psychoanalytic approach for the analysis. In the end, the theory and method of analysis are motivated by a question, which, for me, is simply discovering the specific narrative strategies used in a set of films to represent India and Indians on the Western movie screen.

For my purpose, when considering narrative strategies, I rely primarily on the work of scholars who would belong to the general

---

[3] Ibid.

area of cultural studies. Scholars, such as John Fiske[4] and John Hartley, developed the theoretical positions offered by thinkers such as Stuart Hall and Louis Althusser to argue that the socially situated texts of film and television offer an open-ended opportunity for "reading." The specific strategies of reading the text are also predicated by the position a reader may take along an ideological continuum, where those embedded within the dominant way of thinking within a society would read the text exactly the way in which the author intended the text to me read. Since the author of the text also works within the dominant way of thinking, often also called the ideological system, the dominant reading of a text aligns with its intended meaning. On the other end of the continuum is the condition where the reader is in complete opposition with the dominant ideology and thus would read the text in a manner that is completely different from the way it was meant to be read. Many different studies have demonstrated this phenomenon, suggesting that texts are inscribed with specific ideological indicators which become evident in a careful analysis of the text where the specific methods of constructing the text become the clues for the analyst to uncover what ideological imperatives dominate the specific construction of the text and the representation it produces and circulates.

This form of analysis also assumes that texts, such as film and TV, are the products of deliberate representational choices made by the authors. Having worked with a documentary filmmaker, it became quickly evident to me that the numerous hours of interviews, location shots, background shots, and so on would certainly make it to the final 30-minute documentary, but Kim, my student and a documentarian, makes a set of choices which determines what specific narrative elements will actually be on the screen. This is a process that is repeated in the construction of most of the films and television shows. In the end, it is important to see what specific choices were made to uncover why they were made. It is by finding the answer to the "why" question is it possible to accurately gauge the way in which India and people from India are represented on the Western screen. It is important to know that Indians are represented as "brown" people in numerous images of

---

[4] John Fiske, *Television Culture* (London: Routledge, 1987).

the West, but it is also important to note that this is done because, for a vast portion of the Western audience, the natural, conventional, and ideologically dominant way to think about Indians is indeed as brown-skinned people. This conclusion is not meant to question the authenticity of the dominant ideological position, but to point toward the mechanisms that operate in informing the representation choices.

Much of the focus for the next two chapters is on the representational choices made by the film and TV industry of the West to offer specific representations. This chapter considers a set of films made in the period of 2001–2014 to discover the strategies of representation and then place them within specific groups to demonstrate how they become mechanisms of creating a specific image of India and people from India. To start with, it is useful to consider how Indian stars become a narrative strategy in producing the image.

INDIAN STARS ON THE WESTERN SCREEN

The Indian movie industry—known as Bollywood since the late 1990s—has a history similar to the Hollywood industry with each having its phases emphasizing systems of production where the producing studio or the stars became the focus of the industry. Indeed, since the mid-1970s, the Bollywood system has become increasingly star centric, where specific names of actors have played an important role in the popularity of the films. With time, these names have changed, but the screens in India have been replete with screen icons that tend to play similar roles in different movies, carving out space for themselves, building a personal brand and genre around the star. One such star has been Amitabh Bachchan, who gained popularity in the 1970s, playing the role of an "angry young man," who takes it upon himself to provide his personal brand of justice, often involving a significant amount of violence to the "bad guys" of the world. Only on the rare occasions did the star play the "bad guy." He became the iconic good person doing the right things for the world around him. It is this star that was transported to the Western screen in Baz Luhrmann's 2013 rendering of *The Great Gatsby* where this Bollywood star was cast with the Hollywood stars such as Leonardo DiCaprio. However, the casting was provocative because the quintessential hero of Bollywood became the villain of

Image 4.1. Screen Capture from *The Great Gatsby* (2013, Released by Warner Brothers and Roadshow Entertainments) which Features Indian Actor Amitabh Bachchan Playing the Role of the Jewish Businessman Meyer Wolfshiem

Courtesy: Author.

Hollywood, playing the role of Meyer Wolfsheim—the Jew in the novel of F. Scott Fitzgerald. In his book, the author of the novel, on which the 2013 movie is based, showed his distaste of the Jews in writing the book in 1925 when many in the West were displaying signs of anti-Semitism. Indeed, in the book, the person played by Amitabh Bachchan is referred to by another character in the novel as "the kike"—an especially pejorative term for Jews. The star of Bollywood becomes the "kike" of Hollywood. Although there are some commentaries that attempt to uncover the rationale leading to this choice, it is important to note that the way a Bollywood film star appears on the Western screen is not at all close to what the star signified in the country of origin. On the other hand, it served the dominant narrative purpose of the Western narrative on the Western screen for the Western audience to see the Indian face where ethnicities are collapsed, and it is decided that a normal way to display the character of which Fitzgerald[5] wrote, "A small, flat-nosed Jew raised his large head and regarded me with two fine growths of hair which luxuriated in either nostril. After a moment I discovered his tiny eyes in the half-darkness."

This is what Hollywood makes of Amitabh Bachchan who has also been described by renowned French filmmaker, Francois

---

[5] Scott Fitzgerald, *The Great Gatsby*, 1925.

Image 4.2. Screen Capture from *Mission Impossible: Ghost Protocol* (2011, Released by Paramount Pictures) which Features Indian Actor Anil Kapoor Playing the Role of Indian Businessman Brij Nath

Courtesy: Author.

Truffaut,[6] as a "one man industry!" This recasting of an Indian star is being witnessed elsewhere as well, where the Indian star becomes the representation of what is outside of the realms of the "normal" within the way meanings are made in the West. It is a tendency which is often seen when an Indian protagonist is needed within the narrative and an Indian star is selected to serve that specific narrative function.

While Luhrmann utilizes an Indian star to play a non-Indian role, in the 2011 *Mission: Impossible–Ghost Protocol*, Brad Bird introduces the key Indian character as, "Brijnath, playboy, multi-media tycoon" who has built an "illegally acquired Cold War castoffs" that includes sophisticated technology to start a nuclear war. Operating out of Mumbai in India, this person is played by another Indian actor, Anil Kapoor, also a star of Bollywood who generally plays the "good guy" in Bollywood, much like Amitabh Bachchan. However, the same actor, when cast with Tom Cruise and Paula Patton of Hollywood, uses the cliché, "I would like to show you my collection of art," and describes himself to the female protagonist by stating, "I am hot. Like all Indian men (sic) are very hot," stating the last "hot" in a drawn out slur. Yet this "hot" Indian male is quickly disabled by the American female agent played by Paula Patton when Anil Kapoor invokes the ancient Indian Tantric language to fondle the female IMF agent.

---

[6] Francois Truffaut.

Image 4.3. Screen Capture from *Pink Panther 2* (2009, Released by Columbia Pictures) which Features Indian Actress Aishwarya Rai Bachchan Playing the Role of Sonia Solandres, the Former Girlfriend of the Villian

Courtesy: Author.

The tendency to cast an Indian star as the Indian protagonist has typically been applied to create a specific image of Indians on the Western screen that remains aligned with the generic expectations of the audience of the West who have been trained to view India and Indians through stereotypical lenses that resonate with the dominant way of thinking about India. Generally, there are, therefore, two different representational strategies used when an Indian star is portrayed on the Western screen—either the star is used to play an "abnormal" function in the narrative or the star represents an Indian in the narrative who is always and already abnormal. Indeed, the need for the Indian star is predicated on the fact that the narrative, in its unique way, offers something out of the ordinary. Consider, for instance, Ang Lee's Oscar-winning *Life of Pi*, released in 2012, which is based on Yann Martel's provocative novel where four different Indian actors represent the various stages of the life of the protagonist with the Indian star Irrfan Khan being the adult version of the protagonist who describes himself as named after a swimming pool. Even though this is from the adaptation of the book, it remains the case that for the many viewers of the Western screen, who were unfamiliar with the book, the Indian on the screen, played again by an Indian star, is indeed portraying an Indian person named after a swimming pool. While this is a distillation of one specific aspect of the movie, the tendency to utilize Indian stars in very specific ways continues here as in some of the other examples.

The utilization of Indian stars on the Western screen is not restricted to male stars. After Aishwarya Rai (Bachchan) was awarded Miss World in 1994, she began to be seen through the Western lens. It was, however, in 1999 that Rai came to fame with *Hum Dil De Chuke Sanam*—a Bollywood blockbuster that utilized Rai's dancing skills also made her famous as an actress against Bollywood actors Salman Khan and Ajay Devgn. Yet it was not until 2004 that Rai was cast as an Indian woman who fell in love with a Caucasian man and the issues that followed. Based loosely on Jane Austen's book, the film *Bride and Prejudice* presents the Indian superstar in a relatively stereotypical Indian-woman depiction who initially takes on the role of the Indian woman helping the White man negotiate India and then she finds herself negotiating America. The movie was made by a person of Indian origin and thus allowed the Indian stars to represent Indians in the way Bollywood might have. But when the same Rai was cast in the 2009 *Pink Panther 2*, the Indian star was modified to fit the Western screen. Here, the same Rai is a villain, similar to Amitabh Bachchan in *The Great Gatsby*, and is the one who seduces the protagonist. Here, too, the Indian star plays a role that is contrary to the accepted place of the star in Bollywood where she has played a series of roles as the demure housewife in *The Raincoat* to the seductive thief in *Dhoom 2*. When presented on the Western movie screen, however, she continues to be mobilized as the non-White slightly strange woman who remains outside of the normal.

The notion of normal is an important component of the imaging of India on the Western screen when the very place becomes something that is a spectacle for the Western audience, many of whom will never actually experience India at all. As I noted in my earlier book, India is exotic and wild, it is a place made up of jungles—both natural and concrete—where danger looms everywhere, and the role of the Western protagonist is indeed to protect the people in the place. This notion is continued in two different ways. First, when India is a part of the narrative arc and it is represented in a specific way. Second, when the narrative arc requires representing a dangerous place, India proves to be an easy choice.

In many cases, however, the Western audience has little knowledge that the dangerous place they see on the screen is India until that information is revealed in the texts that surround the original movie—such as a well-written review of the movie.

WHAT INDIA LOOKS LIKE ON THE WESTERN MOVIE SCREEN

In the opening of the second movie of the Bourne trilogy, we are presented with the location of Goa in India where the protagonist Jason Bourne is hiding out with his partner. This, however, is a much nuanced representation of Goa, which is considered by many to be an international beach destination much like the destinations in the Caribbean. In *The Bourne Supremacy*, which is based on the Robert Ludlum spy thrillers, Goa is a jungle where Jason Bourne is the hunted and Goa becomes the place where his girlfriend is killed by the villain who turns out to be a Russian. India is the killing field. What is interesting to note is the internationalization of the space, where the battle is in India but between enemies who are not necessarily Indians. In a similar turn of events in *Mission: Impossible–Ghost Protocol*, Tom Cruise leads his band of spies to India, where again the battle is between the character played by Tom Cruise and villains from Russia. As pointed out earlier in this chapter, the Indian villain is easily subdued by the Western woman, but it requires battling the true villains in the multistory parking lot of Mumbai. The Western movie screen brings India to the cineplexes of the West and represents the space as one that is fraught with dangers, and often the place where opposing forces might clash while the Indians on the screen are mere spectators. I continue to characterize this depiction as evocative of the "jungle" metaphor—a place composed of the predator and the hunted where India becomes the appropriate site to depict the conflict. Needless to say, many other places have been represented in this manner. The gangster movies of Hollywood, ranging from the well-known Godfather trilogy to even obscure gangland movies have also depicted many American spaces as the jungle, but there have been alternative representations as well. However, for India on the hand, the most popular representation that has been circulated widely on the Western screen is a place that is "dangerous" and "ruthless" to the ones that have to inhabit it.

The notions of danger have been well developed in many of the films to depict that danger is expressed in many different ways. In the *Best Exotic Marigold Hotel* of 2011, the danger lies in many different places from the way in which the protagonist, a person who is running a rickety old mansion as a hotel populated by elderly guest from England, has to stave off his own mother from ruthlessly smashing his dreams. In this case, the protagonist and the mother are both Indians but, nevertheless, the place turns out to be dangerous for the protagonist. In a creative way, the narrative of the Marigold Hotel normalizes and circulates a narrative where the place is an urban jungle—chaotic and colorful—but with an innate danger that can eventually entrap a person as in the case of one of the protagonists whose desire to leave the place is so strong that she is willing to take a rickshaw through the streets of Jaipur to get to the airport and depart. The representation of the place remains quite in line with the earlier representations where India is only a stopping point, a place where the protagonists would never stay forever. At the same time, the Marigold Hotel also offers an internally contradictory representation of place because, unlike many other movies, here in John Madden's *Best Exotic Marigold Hotel*, there are a few who were sufficiently transformed by the place that they decided to stay. As in many cases, such internal contradictions within the narrative can begin to transform the way the place is being represented. Other movies could begin to offer the "other" representation of the

Image 4.4. Screen Capture from *Best Exotic Marigold Hotel* (2012, Released by Fox Searchlight Pictures) which Features India as the Setting for the Narrative

Courtesy: Author.

place that transcends from being the jungle or the temporary stopping point to becoming more of a destination where protagonists stay. Such a representation would begin to question what has been the dominant representation of the place on the Western screen.

Yet such alternative representations are only seen in limited movie screens of the West. For instance, the representation of the place is quite complex in the 2007 Wes Anderson film called *The Darjeeling Limited* which brings together an odd crew of actors who travel through India as they rediscover themselves and eventually meets their mother who has chosen India as a destination to be a nun at a Christian abbey in India. Even though a Western protagonist would have limited narrative opportunities of being placed permanently in India, the representation of the Caucasian woman in an abbey mimics the reality of people, such as Mother Teresa—a Western person who did the work of Christ in India. These representations struggle to find an ideological place where it remains within the conventional representation while advancing a narrative arc that offers the opportunity of locating a Westerner in India—living well—in spite of being in the jungle. Unfortunately, the Western screen does not offer too many opportunities for these representations since movies like *The Darjeeling Limited* are often too limited in their reach and do not remain on the Western screen for too long—frequently relegated to the "art theaters" before being distributed for the TV screen. On the other hand, movies with large reach continue to propagate the myth of the jungle even if there is some resistance to that representational strategy.

The jungle becomes the dominant image in the opening scenes of the 2012 international blockbuster called *The Avengers*—a story about the superheroes who save Earth from evil powers. One of these heroes is seen in India—specifically the slums of Calcutta—living out the alter-ego life as a doctor treating leprosy. In an intertextual arc—that connects many narratives through leprosy—this representation of India seamlessly connects images from movies like *City of Joy* (1992) to movies like *Slumdog Millionaire* (2008). The "slum and leprosy" become the dominant representation of the space on the Western screen.

What is important to note in these representations is the recurring question of authenticity. Is the space depicted on the

Western movie screen, indeed, like the "real" space that only a small portion of the audience will ever see? The answer to this question offers a point of discussion about the way in which the image is constructed and distributed, but it does not detract from the fact that the representation has always and already been distributed. After that, the representation becomes more powerful from any other reality that could have been represented, but a specific choice was made to keep the other images absent from the screen and the Western gaze at the body of India—in all its perverse pleasures—become the dominant gaze at India. In the next section, I consider two movies which offer examples of how the notions of stars and settings come together to offer an India on the Western screen.

SLUMDOG MILLIONAIRE

No discussion of the image of India on the movie screens of the West would be complete without examining the winner of the Academy Award for Best Picture of 2009. The movie is focused on the lives of two boys from the slums of Bombay who take their destinies in different directions. One of the boys ends up participating in a popular TV show in India that promises the winner of a quiz contest a total of one million Rupees. The young contestant draws upon his life experiences to answer the questions, where the experiences have been of an underdog in the slums of Bombay. Thus, as the maker of the movie, Danny Boyle pointed out the name slumdog—a play on the word underdog.

The fact that the director acknowledges that the narrative is indeed of an underdog who must pull out of the oppressive situation in life is a good reminder that this movie lines up alongside many other narratives where the Indian underdog becomes the primary theme. It is this underdog who is again placed in the jungle that is India, and there must be a series of people who will assist the underdog to become a millionaire. Much like earlier narratives such as the *City of Joy* (1992), the narrative of the Indian in the slum is replicated where the rickshaw puller of the slums of Calcutta is replaced by the children of slums of Bombay. This focus on the slums has been the primary argument that was presented in academic and popular forums after the release of the movie, and especially after its success with the Awards. There was a significant amount of commentary in the popular press that ranged from discussions on how the movie was exploiting the poverty of India by calling upon the perverse pleasures of watching squalor to sell tickets and gain accolades to the way in which the movie could act as an advocate for the poor in the slums of Bombay. In terms of the latter hope, there was some noticeable increase in the interest of the "slum tours" for tourists visiting Bombay.[7]

The discussion about the movie happened on many different forums—from the newspapers of India to film magazines all over the world. I was approached by several news outlets and was asked about my opinion on the movie. One of the things that was noticeable among the non-Indian journalists was the fact that many considered the movie to be an Indian movie synonymous with Bollywood movie—as if the movie was made by an Indian moviemaker for the Indian audience. The fact that the question was raised by many is an especially important moment about the way in which stars and places were utilized to represent Indian on the Western screen through this movie.

A majority of the actors in the movie were Indian stars playing Indian roles. It was a move away from the tendency of Indian stars standing in for other nationalities. Both the good and evil in the movie were played by Indian stars, some of whom are well-known Bollywood actors. It created a sense that it was, indeed, an Indian movie. That notion was further strengthened by the fact that the place was indeed India. It was not a location that was standing in for a different place as discussed earlier, but the atrocities one was witnessing were happening in the slum that is India—leading undoubtedly to the increased traffic in the slum tourism. These two elements of the movie further helped to transfer the ownership of the narrative and the representation away from a Western director,

---

[7] http://www.tandfonline.com/doi/abs/10.1080/17513057.2010.533785#.U42jfvldU4I
http://www.tandfonline.com/doi/abs/0.1080/09528822.2010.491379#.U42j7_ldU4I
http://eprints.lse.ac.uk/29542/
http://bcq.sagepub.com/content/73/2/150.extract
http://jcl.sagepub.com/content/46/2/311.shortce
http://link.springer.com/article/10.1007/s10708-010-9401-7
http://www.tandfonline.com/doa/abs/10.1080/01436591003701117#.U42mxfldU4I
http://en.wikipedia.org/wiki/Controversial_issues_surrounding_Slumdog_Millionaire
http://www.boxoffice.com/articles/2010-02-another-bollywood-hit

making yet another movie about the slum-based underdog of India. Instead, when the stars show up on the Western screen placed in the accepted version of the representation of the Indian space, serenaded by the familiar strains of Indian music, the audience could easily believe that this is the "real" India since it is an Indian movie that must be accurate about what India looks like. By removing the familiar non-Indian, often White, savior from the narrative and the Western screen, the movie gained a sense of authenticity and was able to shed the White responsibility of saving the underdog, thus firmly confirming that the movie was about India made by Indians.

The movie entered the popular cultural space as an Indian movie and not many actually realized that it was selected as the best picture in the 2009 Oscars as the best picture of the year and not in the category of "foreign films." It was the brilliance of the movie because it represented India with the use of a narrative; here, it utilized the stars, the place, and a set of narrative strategies that was different from the way all of the same elements have been used in other movies that bring India to the Western movie screen. The adaptation of the elements of Bollywood, as in the case of the closing scenes of the Jay Ho dance which replicated the Bollywood look using the music of one of the stars of Bollywood music. This set of strategies used to make the movie appear to be Indian actually allowed to naturalize the image of India. The concern with the Western gaze at India was replaced by the sense that it was the image of India as seen through the eyes of an Indian and brought to the screen by Indian stars. No other movie that has represented India has been able to hide the author as well as this movie did, thus, ascribing the ideological stance of the movie to Indians bringing India to the Western screen as opposed to a Western author imaging of India. This duplicity was much less evident in the other movie that I discuss here where the Western audience watching the Western screen was never confused about the author—Disney.

MILLION DOLLAR ARM

In 2014, Disney studios released a movie that was described by some commentators as "Fun, Family-Friendly Flick."[8] The

---

[8] http://www.huffingtonpost.com/lonna-saunders/million-dollar-arm-family_b_5429853.html

movie also rightfully claimed to be based on real events and real people and was brought to the Western screen as a movie about baseball—one of the most valuable American pastimes. In fact, when I asked some of my undergraduate students about the movie, many thought of it as a "baseball movie," as opposed to a movie where India was a significant part of the narrative.

It was one of the few movies that arrived on the Western screen with no pretenses about how the country and the people would be portrayed while using the same semantic elements of the star and place. In this case, the stars represented Indians who were non-fictional, and the places were "real." Being based on real life events and people, the movie had both representational restrictions and latitude. The authors could not conjure up imaginary places that could be a representation of India, neither could they represent on the Western screen people who did not appear authentic. This restricted the nature of the representations to what could be believable as India and Indians. Yet it was also the source of the latitude in representation since the authors were immune from criticism from the audience of the Western screen of manipulating the images to suit the narrative functions that have been commonplace in the representation of India and Indians. There was no ideological guilt in representing Indians as the ones being "saved" from the squalor and destitution of their rural Indian existence by being transported to Los Angeles. The recurring binary connection between the White Savior and the Brown Saved was indeed the "truth." In representing this, the authors merely had to draw upon a series of existing representational strategies such as the White protagonist—the baseball agent—reassuring the mother of one of the Indian recruits that her son would be "safe" with the agent in America, literally offering the role of the "savior" to the agent.

While this movie stays within most of the representational boundaries, it also indicates how movies and texts become internally controversial as many different tendencies influence the way in which Indians could be represented on the Western screen. Being a Disney movie, there was a certain responsibility to remain within the broader American ideological practices that would attempt to remind the audience the importance of "family," "relationships," "love," and especially an ending, or narrative closure, that would remain in alignment with the dominant ideological position for a society at any moment in time. It has been argued by cultural and critical scholars that the narrative closure is an important indicator of the way in which the hegemonic order of things are neatly maintained in the way the story ends. In the case of this movie, the closure had to not only remain true to the story but also offer the Disney-like ending. Here, too, reality helped, because the recruits were indeed successful in their endeavors. However, the representation of the people from India left the trodden path because the binary relationship between the savior and the saved was reversed and the three Indian boys eventually "saved" the agent from a life of loneliness and despair. The Indians not only pitch in an acceptable way but they also show the agent the power of religious prayer and need for familial connection to be successful and happy in life. The traditional representational strategies connected with India, yoga, for instance, is not used as a marker of being Indian but as a tool that would allow for attaining the sense of peace that the baseball agent so needed.

It is important to note that this film uses representational strategies which are not very different from those used by many of the other films mentioned in this discussion. Furthermore, there are many more films which use the strategies discussed here and nearly all of the other narratives remain within the generic and formulaic modes of representation discussed. This intertextual similarity helps to make some images and representations natural to the audience of the Western screen. Scholars of genre studies of films have pointed out that it is the similarity in the modes of representation that allow films to be classified into genres, just as the knowledge that a film belongs to a genre allows the audience to make sense of the film. Indeed, the audience expects to see India as the jungle and the Westerner as the savior. The *Million Dollar Arm* offers a certain interruption to that generic representation. In this case, the movie alters the narrative sufficiently to call into question the "natural" and "conventional" representations of India and the people from India. The film maintains sufficient closeness with what the audience would expect to see—the squalor of Mumbai, the villages, the awkward Indian in the Los Angeles—but it is also compelled to represent some other aspects of India and Indians which would not be expected in a movie that represents

India. When a movie like this appears in the public sphere, it has the potential to begin to alter the conventional representations and call into question the image of India on the Western movie screen.

NOT MUCH HAS CHANGED

Eventually, looking at the way in which the nation and its people were portrayed in the movies before the 1990s and the movies after the 1990s, there is a scant change in the conventional and natural meanings that are associated with India for a large majority of the audience of the Western screen. Some of the representational strategies have certainly changed. There are more Indian stars on the Western screen now than in the latter part of the twentieth century, and some of them return and can thus be billed as the star of an earlier, sometimes a well-known movie. For instance, in *Million Dollar Arm*, two primary Indian actors have already been seen on the Western screen in the movies *Life of Pi* and *Slumdog Millionaire*. A possible outcome of this recurrence of the Indian star could eventually become commonplace. What would be interesting to observe is what the stars end up representing as I have discussed here.

The use of India as the backdrop of the narrative, where space plays a specific and unique role, also continues much like it did with earlier movies. However, the fact that the landscape in India has changed over time cannot be ignored by the movies. Thus, the squalor of Bombay cannot completely hide the high-rise buildings of the city, nor is it possible to ignore the lavishness of a party organized by an Indian tycoon as in the case of *Mission: Impossible – Ghost Protocol*. This is a space which is no longer the exotic jungle with elephants and snakes, but a place where one can use Voice over Ip, as in the case of Skype, from a hotel room or a place where Indians are ready and willing to call into question the Western ways of doing things as in the case of the call center workers of *Outsourced* or *My Best Exotic Marigold Hotel*. The representation of the place has to look different simply based on the changes that are happening in the real place, but the meaning associated with the place often has to remain what it has been for many years.

While much of the representational status quo is maintained, the movie screen of the West is being compelled to reconsider the way in which India would be represented because the number of screens has proliferated. For instance, the real life baseball players who make up the narrative of the *Million Dollar Arm* have already appeared on the TV screen of the West when they first played baseball for a national team in America. Such images have circulated on the TV screen at an increasing frequency since the turn of the century. The Western movie screen must compete with the representational strategies of the Western TV screen as well because it is the same audience who is viewing these screens. Thus, it is interesting to examine the India that is seen on the Western TV screen in Chapter 5.

5. THE TELEVISION SCREEN

Television (TV) got a foothold in the Western media space after World War II (WWII) when a couple of different things happened in the West that altered the role of TV and TV screen in the West. The first event was the reconstruction of the media industry in much of Western Europe that remained aligned with the United States. With the beginning of the Cold War, there was a rapid need to rebuild the devastated media infrastructure of countries such as England, France, West Germany, and other parts of Europe that did not fall under the Soviet Block. There was a need to build a distribution system as well as to provide content for TV which would be entertaining to an audience weary after years of war. The second event was the commercial and cultural interests of the USA to offer inexpensive and high-quality TV content for Europe. The American interest was in colonizing the European mind and propagating a free-market economic model based on a democratic form of government. This goal was well fulfilled with the flooding of the European media space with TV programs from America. Many have lamented that this was the moment of rapid Americanization of European media to the benefit of the American TV industry which saw a period of boom after the War. The outcome of these two events was the universalization of what the Western audience viewed on TV—from London to Los Angeles—American TV programs reigned supreme.

Over the years since the War, the TV industry grew rapidly in America with many significant changes to the industry through the adoption of new forms of transmission and the proliferation of content. What used to be regime of a handful of corporations such as National Broadcasting Corporation (NBC), Columbia Broadcasting System (CBS), and a few others grew into a media marketplace of hundreds of broadcasters who sent their content to the consumer using many different technologies such as the ubiquitous cable, satellite, and the Internet. Almost all of the content was, however, commercially funded, leading to a fierce competition for the attention of the "eyeballs" of the audience. The content had to be fragmented and designed for specific segments of the audience with specific tastes making it imperative that the viewer at home had to choose programming based on personal interest leading to a need for multiple TV screens at home. Different members of a traditional American household, for instance, would have their "personal" TV in their personal space where they would watch their favorite shows which might not necessarily be appealing to other members of the household. This fragmentation of content and segmentation of the audience led to a condition where the number of screens in a home continued to grow as well. Indeed, in 2006, it was reported that an average American home has more TV screens than people at home.[1] The TV screen appeared in many different spaces from the inside of a public transport to waiting areas at hospitals. By 2014, the Western audience was constantly surrounded by the TV screen which offered many different options of programming. In this intently competitive space, it was important for content producers to create material that would attract attention from a large audience, thus, garnering higher advertising revenue. Any content that would offer something unique was more likely

---

[1] http://usatoday30.usatoday.com/life/television/news/2006-09-21-homes-tv_x.htm

to become popular and there was a constant quest to find something special that would make the content especial while remaining within the general expectations of the audience. The need to maintain the intricate balance between formulaic familiarity and offering something new partly led to the adoption of people from India and the locale of India as an important part of the TV content in the West, leading to the representation of Indians and India on the TV screen of the West. In this chapter, I point toward some of the ways in which the notion of India was incorporated, especially in the Western TV of the twenty-first century.

WHY INDIA?

The audience of the Western TV screen had grown rapidly after WWII and most of the audience was in the affluent United States that was witnessing the post-War economic boom where Americans were hungry for the consumer goods that were being churned out by the factories of the West. These goods—from automobiles to dishwashing machines—were being sold on the TV screens largely for the White America of the 1950s. The Civil Rights Movement was beginning to take force, but to the American advertiser, the consumer was still primarily the middle-class American family with a working father, a homemaker mother, and the children. For this market, the Western TV screen was mostly concerned with TV shows that would find identification with the consumer of the products making most of the shows based on wholesome family values that represented White, homogeneous America. From the evening family shows to the afternoon soap operas, the Western TV screen did not have to deal with the diversity of races and opinions. In fact, it was in 1965 that Bill Crosby, an African-American entertainer, appeared in an action-adventure TV show called *I Spy*. Notably, this came two years after Martin Luther King Jr, the African-American civil right leader in the USA, delivered his famous "I have a dream" speech demanding the end to racism in the United States. Through the 1970s and 1980s, there was an increasing disappearance of the visible face of racism and the African-American minority in America became an important segment of the audience of TV in the USA and, thus, found increasing presence on the TV screen of the West, albeit in very specific ways that represented a specific image of the African-American.

The history of appearance of the African-American on the Western screen is informative about the way in which a particular race appears on the Western TV, especially when the race does not represent the author of the narrative of the screen. In most of the cases, until stars such as African-American talk show host Oprah Winfrey begin their own programs, they were represented by others who would place them in a specific role motivated by the decisions of the author—who often was not African-American. This process also happened with people from India. When the Indian minority in diaspora in the West becomes a player in the economic and social space of the West, the Indian begins to appear on the Western screen—placed there and represented by non-Indian authors. In those conditions of representation and production, certain specific images begin to emerge that retain a very well-defined position for the Indian on the Western screen.

TV'S FICTIONAL INDIAN

The confusion about bringing in a South Asian character in a popular TV show begins from the time when the character of Babbu Bhatt was introduced in the episode called *The Café* in the popular TV show *Seinfeld* in November 1991. This particular person is the quintessential South Asian, in this case, evidently from Pakistan, who represents the entrepreneurial spirit of the community who is eventually misled by the protagonist, Jerry Seinfeld. The fact that Babbu is the product of a Western author is evident in the confusion over basic identity creation such as naming a person from Pakistan—made up of a population of Muslims—with a typically Hindu name, which is very far from the reality of being a Pakistani in America. On the Western screen, the name and the character conflate into an aberrational representation which would be confusing to any informed viewer, but would look quite "normal" to the viewer of the Western screen. In many ways, the character becomes less important than the specific tendencies the person represents— attempting to camouflage the real identity of the diasporic entrepreneur who sets up an Italian café; whereas, the person's real strength lies in Pakistani cuisines. This character brings to the screen the elements that have defined the South Asian immigrant who must abandon the original identity narrative to adopt the new

Image 5.1. A Screenshot from *Seinfeld* (Season 3, Episode 7), a Show on American Network Channel NBC that Features a South Asian Protagonist

Courtesy: Author.

narrative offered in the New World. This is the expected position of the Indian or Pakistani on the Western screen. Other options are relegated to failure as is the case with Babbu whose later attempt to convert the Italian cafe, based on advice from Jerry, results in complete disaster, eventually leading up to events where the immigrant meets the fate of failure—deportation from the USA.

The representation of the immigrant Indian as somewhat aberrational with peculiarities that are only attributed to the fact of being Indian is replicated many years later on the Western screen again in *The Big Bang Theory* that aired in 2007. The show chronicles the life of four scientists who are good friends with two of them living in an apartment complex where their next door neighbor is a waitress at a local restaurant and clearly without the academic credentials of the scientist quartet. The comedic element of the show is derived principally from the idiosyncrasies of each character which are intimately tied to the conventional imaginations of scientists and waitresses. The scientists revel in their brand of "nerdom" while the "blond waitress" offers the counterpoint to the "intelligence" of the scientists. Two of the scientists

Image 5.2. A Screenshot from *The Big Bang Theory* (Series 7, Episode 3), a Show on American Network Channel ABC that Features an Indian Protagonist

Courtesy: Author.

also represent the two major minority populations in the USA—Jews and Indians. Both these groups are already and always well known for their academic and economic achievements, and thus the identities are well created by offering the characters names that are undeniably Jewish and Indian—mechanical engineer Howard Wolfowitz and astrophysicist Raj Koothrappali. Additionally, as the show progresses there are some other Indian characters introduced in the show, most notably, Raj's sister—Priya.

In this narrative, there is again a need to define the Indian character around specific and "expected" traits which all set aside Raj as uniquely Indian. This Indian speaks with the accent that must sound Indian—a task done brilliantly by the actor Kunal Nayar. The aberration, in this case, is defined around the fact that the Indian scientist is too bashful and is unable to talk to women. It becomes the defining characteristic of the person offering a representation of the "dorky" Indian super intelligent scientist at a prestigious research institute in the USA working on advanced problems in astrophysics but unable to hold a conversation with an American waitress at a restaurant. The character must depend on his American friends to be able to negotiate simple conversations with women but at the same time, he is not without the quintessential libido and the desire for the Western White woman. In the episode where Penny, the waitress, and Raj find themselves in bed together, the viewer of the Western screen is reassured that "nothing happened" and the place of the Indian male is reconstructed as the somewhat impotent person who may desire but may not reach. This motif of sexuality of Raj is reversed in the case of his sister who is much more of the Indian woman—sensual and exotic—as much the object of the desire of the Western male as the Western woman is of the Indian male. The difference is the fact that the Indian woman is much more open to the approaches of the Western male, and even "Internet sex" with networked kissing tools becomes fair game in the representation of the Indian woman.

Such representations of the Indian on the Western TV screen resonate with the representations seen elsewhere on other screens such as the movie screen. There is, however, one significant point of difference—the Indian on the Western TV screen is also most often and Indian placed within the cultural space of the West. For instance, it is no longer the case that the Indian male is desirous of the Western woman when the woman is in the cultural space of India; rather, the Indians are now a part of the Western space and, thus, the actions are of particularly special import because it reminds the viewer of the Western TV screen what the Indian looks like in the real world of the viewer. The Western screen now becomes the site where the Indian comes alive with all the characteristics that would be sought in an Indian who the audience encounters "off screen." In some ways, this is how stereotypes are produced and circulated, but the process is far more efficient here since it is not only the characterization based on some broad demographic strokes but is based on a character in a popular show who consistently presents the Indian self in the Western space. This mechanism makes the Indian scientist more "believable" as an Indian in *The Big Bang Theory,* just as the Indian office worker comes alive in the character of Kelly Kapoor in *The Office.* Watching the portrayal of the rather confused and awkward character in the show, it would be impossible to reconcile the facts that the person Mindy Kaling, also an accomplished actor, writer, and director, who has won awards for co-creating the character in the show, stays in contrast to the person who plays the character. It is true for the world of entertainment for the most performers. The

Image 5.3. A Screenshot from *The Office*, a Show on American Network
Channel NBC that Features an Indian Protagonist

Courtesy: Author.

stage persona does not usually reflect the actual person, as it should
not. However, in the case of characters such as Raj and Kelly, these
characterizations are the ones that become the dominant ways of
considering the Indian on the Western screen when placed in the
Western space. Thus, Mindy is not only the one who says, "I talk
a lot, so I've learned to just tune myself out," but is also the waitress in the film *Unaccompanied Minors*, and a museum tour guide
in the film, *Night at the Museum: Battle of the Smithsonian*. She
breaks out of these portrayals only as a physician in *No Strings
Attached*, a film where she acts as the roommate of the protagonist.

These different ways in which the Indian person is inserted
in the Western fictional space, shown on the TV screens of the
West, is complemented in the nonfictional spaces created by
the Western TV screen. It is the space that is created through
the mushrooming of cable channels with special interest that
offer a look at India through narrative formats that stretch from
the "reality" shows such as *An Idiot Abroad* to the more somber
and believable documentaries offered by providers such as the
National Geographic and Public Broadcasting Systems (PBS) such
the British Broadcasting Corporation (BBC) of Britain or PBS in
America. It is a genre of TV shows that deserve attention since

there is an increasing availability and interest in such TV shows that transports the Western viewer to the "real" India of the "real" Indian as opposed to the Indian working in an American office.

TV'S REAL INDIA

India has been the subject of the documentary lens of a variety of people and institutions, and the images have eventually shown up on the Western TV screens as the viewers have attempted to both learn about India and be amused by what they are watching. There is a great deal of variety in such programming that includes the well-respected and widely viewed *The Story of India* by Michael Woods to the more lighthearted and amusing episodes from shows such as *An Idiot Abroad* or the long-running American TV show called *The Amazing Race*.

The representation created by these nonfictions programming on the Western TV screen attempt to bring the "real" India and the "real" Indian to the audience. In most of the cases, the representation is consumed by people who will actually never experience India but attribute conditions and qualities that are shaped by the various screens. Within this shape, India appears as an ancient country with practices and rituals that are so far removed from the West which automatically becomes exoticized. There are, however, two common themes related to the notion of ancient as the age is represented by the things that Indians do, that is, their cultural practices, and the places that make up India, such as temples and caves. Modern India is relegated out of the screen space other than as a contrast to what was the gorgeous past as compared to the crumbling present with the hint of an uncertain future.

Consider, for instance, the opening of the Michael Woods' work. Within the first 60 seconds of the first episode, we are confronted with images of a temple, a Mughal palace, and the Taj Mahal along with scenes of rural India. This is followed by the montage of shots of India Gate and Jama Masjid in Delhi, and the images of a road and cars speeding by along with the images of a religious ceremony. The voice over posits the theme of the show by concluding with the statement, "one of the greatest players in history is rising again." Such an opening clearly emphasizes that the primary claim for India is indeed its history. The documentary is replete with the images of the "old": the ancient archeological digs of the Indus Valley Civilization and the chanting of a sect of little-known Brahmanic priests of the southern coastal state of Kerala. Even in the conclusion of the six-part series the screen is filled with the images of the onion domes of the Jama Masjid where Mr Woods praises the country for possessing a "cultural immune system" that allows India to draw upon its history of cultures to survive and flourish. Here, the places of history and the practices, primarily religious, frame the nation and its people. In a much more light-hearted way, these themes are replicated in other non-fiction that appears on the Western TV screen.

In a self-reflexive moment of being Western—a British man in this case—the producers of *An Idiot Abroad* demonstrates what happens to the common Western man when confronted with different cultures. Being called a "practical joke," the show places the same individual in China, Egypt, and India among other places in the world. In the second season of the show, when the visit to India was aired, the show had nearly 1.3 million viewers in the UK, and thereafter, more in other parts of the world. On the screen, India came to these viewers as a country of ancient traditions and squat-type bathrooms which one Indian describes to the protagonist as, "It is better," while the London-reared protagonist is overwhelmed by the chaos of Delhi. The audience, sitting in the comfort of the semi-detached in Wandsworth and other such places, is equally aghast at the plight of the protagonist. Even though the protagonist is described as a typical British, who is sent out of a "comfort zone," the exact same thing happens for the viewers of the screen, who would conclude that the image of India is indeed one of "there is shit everywhere," as the protagonist declares standing at a busy street corner of an unidentified Indian city. The rationale for the experience is, however, embedded in what Michael Woods offers—history and the fact that India is an ancient country.

The age of the country is connected quite distinctly with the religions of the country and the practices related to religion. In most of the documentaries and nonfiction about India, the Western screen is replete with images that remind the viewer that the key cultural practices of the country and the most important places and events are connected to a myriad of religions. Consider the way in which Michael Woods talks of the sculptures on a Hindu temple pointing out that sculptures represent the hundreds of thousands of Indian Gods stating, "Why have only one God when you can have thousands?" This contrast with the Western experiences of monotheism emphasizes that, as an old civilization, India remains a place where the ancient practices continue uninterrupted, making the place distinctly different from the lived experience of the majority of the people who are watching the Western TV screen. In some cases, there is a little contextualization of the practices and they are almost depicted as unexplained acts that simply remain exotic to the Western protagonists of the nonfiction programs collapsing the bewilderment of the protagonists with the puzzlement of the millions of viewers of the Western TV screen. When the "idiot" of the BBC show states on camera, "Every time we stop someone slaps me with a lot of colors," the entire tradition of the Holi Festival is reduced to an unexplained ritual that is encapsulated in the statement, "I don't know what's going on." It becomes the representation of the nation as the images show animals and people covered with the colored powder that defines the experience of Holi in India. The lack of explanation of the event or the idiot's disinterest in attempting to understand what is going on replicates the consistent position that it is impossible to understand the country other than by explaining what is going on by relying on the underlying theme that things in India are best explained by its age.

Within that construction of the nation, many things remain off screen where alternative images and explanations are avoided since they might not fit with what the Western screen must conventionally depict for its audiences. It is precisely the argument that thinkers such as Edward Said[2] have proposed that the Western media is still caught in a representational strategy that continues to replicate what the Western authors said about India nearly a century ago. For instance, in writing about Indian customs, Jules Verne[3] mentions the sati in his 1873 book *Around the World in Eighty Days* where the author places his protagonists in the following situation:

---

[2] Said, *Orientalism*.
[3] Jules Verne, *Around the World in Eighty Days* (France: Pierre-Jules Hetzel, 1873).

Sir Francis watched the procession with a sad countenance, and, turning to the guide, said, "A suttee."

The Parsee nodded, and put his finger to his lips. The procession slowly wound under the trees, and soon its last ranks disappeared in the depths of the wood. The songs gradually died away; occasionally cries were heard in the distance, until at last all was silence again.

Phileas Fogg had heard what Sir Francis said, and, as soon as the procession had disappeared, asked: "What is a suttee?"

"A suttee," returned the general, "is a human sacrifice, but a voluntary one. The woman you have just seen will be burned tomorrow at the dawn of day."

"Oh, the scoundrels!" cried Passepartout, who could not repress his indignation.

"And the corpse?" asked Mr. Fogg.

"Is that of the prince, her husband," said the guide; "an independent rajah of Bundelcund."

"Is it possible," resumed Phileas Fogg, his voice betraying not the least emotion, "that these barbarous customs still exist in India, and that the English have been unable to put a stop to them?"

In some ways, this passage is precisely what the idiot of the BBC show expresses to rationalize his experience of a more benign practice of putting color on people for the Holi festival. The Western book of the 1800s and the Western screen of 2000s, both rely on a notion of history to help explain some of what appears before the audience of the Western screens. This overwhelming reliance on the ancient customs to bring India to the screen has thus been a consistently constructed image that has seen wide circulation on the Western nonfiction TV screen.

There are, however, some alternative images that are entering the realm of the Western TV screen. These images are motivated by the imperatives of global capitalism and the recognition that the Western TV screen is no longer the bastion of the Western audience alone who are unaccustomed to India and Indians, but the screen is also the cultural site for the emerging Indian diasporic audience. As pointed out earlier, this audience is an ever growing economic force in the West, and some commercial programs are beginning to bring India to the Western TV screen through the vehicle of a TV advertisement.

COMMERCIALS ON THE WESTERN SCREEN

As discussed in Chapter 2, the Western screen, from the movie screen to the screen of the smartphone, is no longer being consumed only by the Western audience. There is now a growing number of people of Indian origin who are also part of the audience of the Western screen. Even though the audience is not very large in number, this group represents a relatively wealthy segment of consumers with very specific needs which is offered by Western corporations. Furthermore, this group is relatively proud of the heritage of being of Indian origin, and it is in the interest of Western and multinational corporations to offer images and discourses that would resonate with this consumer group.

Remembering that most of these commercials appear during the normal program line-up for prime time TV in the West, it is important to note that these commercials are viewed by a large set of people many of whom would not have any interest in the service being offered, but might have a brand recognition of the service provider. Thus, for most of the audience of the TV screen, these images and discourses serve a function similar to other depictions of India and its people on the TV screen. Yet, because of the specific commercial motive of these images, the depiction of the country and its people stand in contrast to the caricatures of fiction TV and the exoticization of the nonfictional documentaries about India. In the case of the commercial programs, the representation focuses usually on the importance of practices that are not only true for a person from India but could apply well to all audiences. This commercial imperative changes the representation where the Indian is no longer "different" with unique needs, but is normalized into the typical consumer whose needs are similar to the millions other who might be watching the commercial. The Indianness of the commercial program only demonstrates the uniqueness of the company that provides the services by demonstrating how the company is "different" based on the way in which the company utilizes images of India and Indians. It also needs to be noted, that this strategy of incorporating India into the programming is a relatively new process, and it will be some time before this might become more prevalent. This process has also received a little attention from researchers, particularly with respect to people from India, although some observers have noted that there is a growing presence of the "minority" in advertisements as corporations are recognizing that the "minority" is making up a very large segment of the customers.[4] There is, however, a very little presence of people from India in the commercials.

Perhaps, the most notable instances of this strategy of using India in its commercials is Vonage Corporation, which provides international telephone services in the USA and the UK. These advertisements have targeted the Indian diaspora in the West by offering the people inexpensive but reliable telephone service to call India from abroad. The images on the TV screen are no longer of exoticized Indians in a foreign land, but of people who look like any other American family in their American homes talking to people in India. These advertisements utilize the theme of calling India and represent the Indian abroad as someone who is intimately connected to the country of origin leading to the demand for the service the companies provide. This image on the Western screen coincides with the theme of tradition that has been developed elsewhere on the screen, but it "normalizes" that theme by suggesting that the connection with the tradition of the original country is a good and laudable thing, and encourages all viewers, independent of the country of origin, to utilize the services offered by Vonage. The ad closes with the statement "Unlimited calls to India and over 60 other countries." In many of the advertisements, the commercial also claims that the "actor" is a real Vonage customer, and most of the advertisements use the theme of connecting with home and family as the primary selling point of the service. For most of the viewers of these advertisements, the service is of little value since Americans and Britons generally do not need to make unlimited calls to foreign countries. Therefore, the goal of the advertisement, for a large portion of the viewers of this commercial, is to utilize the Indian in the advertisement as a vehicle to sell the brand

---

[4] http://www.slate.com/articles/arts/culturebox/2010/06/beyond_apu.2.html and http://adage.com/article/news/ad-campaigns-finally-reflects-diversity-u-s/292023/

name of the company as opposed to the actual service being advertised. People from India, thus, become brand ambassadors for the
company and the company mobilizes the well-known connection
between India, tradition, and family to promote the brand.

Even though the representation of Indian in the commercials
attempts to make the Indians appear more like other people in
the Western audience, there are some similarities with the overall
image of the Indian on the Western screen. For instance, just as Raj
of *The Bing Bang Theory* regularly stays in touch with his parents
using video calling, the real actor of the commercial also stays in
touch with the family with Vonage service. Through such similarities, the diasporic Indian on the Western TV screen is always and
already has been constructed as someone whose connection with
the country of adoption is always tempered by the connection with
the country of "origin." This is quite in contrast to the history of
immigration in the United States where the country of "origin" for
many European immigrants was left behind. The new immigrants,
especially from India and the "sixty other countries," are represented as different because of their need to stay in connection with
the traditions of the ancient country. The commercial representation does offer an alternative image of the Indian on the screen
but continues to circulate a theme that the general audience of the
Western screen will agree with when it comes to people from India.

THE TV INDIAN ON THE WESTERN SCREEN

As demonstrated here, a set of peculiar contradictions develops
when the Indian is represented on the TV screens of the West. The
person from India is either placed in West or India. Depending on
where the person is, the Indian and India have attributed to a set
of characteristics which serve two purposes, independent of the
geographic location of the narrative. First, the Indian in the West is
held in contrast with the rest of the protagonists in the TV fictions
of the West. The person from South Asia is integrated into the narrative to serve the function of providing a point of contrast to the
other elements in the narrative. It is the contrast that becomes the
point of focus in presenting the Indian. Interestingly, the contrast
is not necessarily one that makes the Indian appear inferior to the
others, but just different. The difference is the focus of presenting

the Indian in the Western fictional TV narrative. It repeats itself across narratives as characters, such as Raj in the show about the physicists, could be remembered as the one who could not speak to women or the Baapu from *Seinfeld* is the one who gets deported because of no fault of his own. In such representations, there is little narrative motivation to present the Indian in the West as someone who is just like the other members of the narrative. It would then perhaps make no sense to include the Indian if indeed the person would be no different from the others.

The Indian in a television narrative that is set in India is quite a different person, thus offering the contrasting and some-times contradictory images and representations about the place and its people on the Western TV screen. To begin with, setting a Western fictional TV series in India is rare and has only been tried once in the West with some degree of success with the series called *Outsourced* that aired on NBC network for one season from September 2010 to May 2011. A similar show called *Mumbai Calling* was aired on BBC and on national public television in Australia in 2009. Neither of the shows lasted for too long, and the American show was cancelled, ostensibly due to lack of popularity, after 22 episodes were aired in the single season of the show. The American show, however, continues to be syndicated to various countries now. These represent situations where the fictional India is brought to the TV screen of the West much in the way the movie screen of the West represented the country and its people. Indeed, the American show was based on a movie of the same name that was released in the USA, without much popularity, in 2006.

The need to set the Indian persons as different from the rest of the protagonists in the narrative becomes more complicated when dealing with shows such as *Outsourced*. The representation of the India in the fiction that is set in India poses a challenge because this person must now be attributed with characteristics that fit the Indian in his own land while contrasting that with the Western in India who, for *Outsourced*, was the primary pro-tagonist. The narrative is built around the plight, challenges, and opportunities that an American faces when he is sent to India to establish a telephone call center and manage a set of Indians who are his employees in India. The Western is, thus, automatically in a position of power in the narrative, whereas Indians in India must work within the differential of power—being subservient to the Western employer as well as being those who support the Western employer to be successful in India. It was a tricky balance in the representational practices since the notion of call centers in India was also a matter of popular and political discussion in the period when the American show was aired. The narrative and the representation of the Indians and India had to remain congruent with the existing "normal" sense of call centers—people with unusual accents trying to sell unnecessary products and services to Americans. The representational juggling to portray the Indian as being "normal" in the Indian space but yet "abnormal" to the Western viewer leads to the second characteristic that can be identified in the representational process which deals with the way the Indian space is represented.

The evidence from the images and narratives continue to produce the space as something completely different from the Western experience. In fiction and nonfiction, the space is exoticized and the practices that are most often represented are remarkably different from what the audience of the Western screen is familiar with. As I have pointed out through examples in this chapter, it is a place whose primary marker is its difference with the West. It is, thus, possible to maintain the notion of difference when placing the Indian person in that space. The Indian protagonist within a narrative set in India appear to act normally within the context of the space that is India but given the fact that the space is always and already differentiated as "strange," the Indian person also becomes the unusual person.

The two primary characteristics of the representation do indeed focus on creating the person and the place as different. It is the celebration and emphasis on the difference from the norms of the West that has continued to define the Indian on the Western TV screen. This tendency has been motivated by the fact that the audience of the Western TV screen has been assumed to be made up of people who are not Indians and, perhaps more importantly, the people who are purchasing products advertised during the shows such as *The Big Bang Theory* are not of Indian origin. This assumption has been increasingly called into question as it has become clear that the miniscule minority that Indians represent in countries like America is an affluent group with large purchasing powers and very specific needs. This is exactly what companies such as Vonage recognize and other institutions are recognizing. Also, the images in the commercials shift away from the other images of Indians on the TV screens of the West.

In addition to the slight shift in the audience of the TV shows, there is a greater shift in the representational dynamics as the movie screen and the TV screen has been supplemented by another emerging screen that is before the audience of the West as well as the audience of the world—the computer screen. As I have suggested earlier, the TV screen and the computer screen has begun to merge into a single screen, but from the analytic perspective, it is important to focus on the computer screen and the way in which the country and its people are represented on that screen.

6. THE COMPUTER SCREEN

The Internet started to become available as a communication tool for the Western population in the late 1990s when people in the West began to realize that the personal computer was not only a machine for professional "work" but also a communication tool that allowed information to stream in on the computer screen. That process was solidified with the developments of the standards that made the Web a part of the everyday life experience of the audience of the West. With these developments, by the early-2000s, there was an additional screen was available to the audience that brought forth a completely different kind of information to the audience—information that defied some of the traditional tenets of mass media, as experienced with the movie screen and the TV screen by changing the nature of the sender of the message as well as altering the nature of the audience.

To understand this change, it is useful to consider some of the basic tenets of mass communication and mass media as historically presented. Most elementary mass media textbooks make the basic assumption that for a form of communication to be classified as mass communication it bears a set of characteristics. First, the message is produced and circulated by an institution as opposed to an individual. Thus, when one thinks of TV news, for instance, the program is created by an institution such as CNN, BBC, or New Delhi Television Limited (NDTV). The message does not have an individual author and is distributed by a network of institutions that could include a satellite broadcaster, a cable TV operator, and other such institutions. Second, the message is distributed and consumed with specific tools, the transmitter and the receiver, at the least. Third, the message is supposed to reach an anonymous and large audience, where the institution might not know who the exact audience member is just as an audience member might not know who the other audience members are. Many of these basic tenets of the mass media are called into question by the digital technologies that allow different ways of message creation and distribution.

To begin with, it is no longer the case that the author of a message needs to be an institution. The early days of the Web witnessed a great interest in the development of personal home pages, where amateur computer programmers were able to rapidly create a presence on Web. Indeed, I still maintain my original Web page that I created in 1994 with the rudimentary coding options available to programmers at that time. Such home pages were individually created, but because of the global distribution of the Internet, a person's home page had the potential of reaching a large anonymous audience where the home page would show up on the computer screen of the individual who might have been "surfing" the Internet. The act of surfing simply involved randomly moving through websites and eventually stumbling upon a website of inter-est. In the development of home page, the Web became a tool of mass communication for the individual, and the computer screen had the opportunity to bring yet another representation of a place and its people. The inclusion of the Web within the list of media of mass communication was heavily debated in the early days of the Web but over time, there was increasing recognition that the computer screen as the conduit for the messages from the Web is a key element of the mass media ecology within which we live now.

With the refinements of the digital technologies, the static website gave way to interactive tools that would make the computer screen a portal into another world, where the "audience" was no longer just the watcher of the representation of a place and its people, but could potentially interact with the people in ways that the movie and TV screens could never permit. These interactions could be of many different kinds, ranging from the sporadic exchange of information through electronic mail or digital social media sites to synchronous interaction with a person where the computer screen would "bring" the other person in the presence of the audience of the Western computer screen. The technological developments were also paralleled by the increasing presence of websites that deal with India. Given the global reach of the Internet and the fact that the presence of the information is purely virtual, it is impossible to accurately state the number of websites about India or the number of websites that have a physical connection with India. It is, however, possible to argue that the number of websites that can show up on a Western screen, which deals with India and its people, is large and growing given that India was the third largest Internet user in the world in 2012, and there are nearly 9 million websites that originate from India. It is these users and the websites that are producing the presence of India on the Western computer screen.

PRESENCE ON THE COMPUTER SCREEN

The type of presence on the computer screen has become increasingly variegated as the digital technology has developed from the early days of the Internet. It is anticipated that the changes will continue as the tools increase and more people have access to the Internet. It is useful to briefly consider the variety of presence that can be found in 2014. I present this along a continuum of interactivity that the Western audience could have with the computer screen.

The commonest form of presence is the traditional static websites that offer information about a place, a person, an institution, or some other aspect of India. It is important to note that such websites do not necessarily have to be created and maintained by people from India. As a matter of fact, these websites could be produced by anyone with access to the Internet and with an interest in India. As I will demonstrate later in this chapter, this kind of websites pose the most challenging analytic situation given the audience of the computer screen might not even have a clear knowledge as to who is offering the representation of the nation and its people.

The second type of presence is the one that offers a clear indication of the author's identity and offers the opportunity to interact with the author through digital discourse. The computer screen brings forth a representation where the author would usually offer sufficient information of personal identity to contextualize the specific representation offered by the website. Furthermore, these websites would allow the viewer to interact with the author to embellish the information available. A blog is a good example of such presence.[1]

The third form of presence takes full advantage of advances in the technology and the computer screen comes alive with the moving image of a person from India who would interact synchronously with the audience. Here, a personal relationship is established between the person of Indian origin and another individual through the conduit of the computer screen, transforming the screen into a two-way communication tool as opposed to the way in which the information is filtered through the screen. Examples of this process are witnessed in the case of web-based tutoring and chat sessions where the user of the screen is connected with the person who appears on the screen. I will discuss this further later in the chapter.

The different forms of presence create different representations and in the next three sections, I examine some of the implications of this variegated presence and the contradictory images that are produced through the process.

STATIC WEBSITE

A static website can be considered to be a digital presence that remains relatively stable and is updated periodically to offer new information as the new information becomes available. It is the typical home page, sometimes also called the "landing page" for a person or an institution. There are many different ways that a Western audience could encounter such a website that deals with India. It is important to note that the way in which the website

---

[1] A blog is a website, often maintained by individuals who log the everyday events of their lives, with appropriate commentary, and then distribution the log over the Internet in the form of web content.

arrives to the Western computer screen has a lot to do with the representation. For this discussion, I focus on three major means by which the website can appear on the screen.

First, the user of the computer screen might have been looking for information about India by entering a term such as "India" in a search engine.[2] It could result in an overwhelming number of responses as millions of websites are listed with the search engine which comes as a result of the search. However, as the search technology stands in 2014, the results that are presented on the screen are often prioritized by the search engine based on the amount of money that a particular website owner has paid to the search engine provider. This is known as the process of search engine optimization (SEO), which is an important tool for digital marketing. Usually, it is institutions with significant funds that are able to pay enough to appear at the top of the list. This inherent bias in search engines creates a specific image of India instantly. For instance, entering the word "India" into several search engines would offer the website of the news institution—Time of India—as one of the top results of the search process. It is the website of an Indian news group and represents an institutional website authored by an institution and housed in India for an audience that will be looking at the website on an Indian computer screen. However, very close to that website are a few other representations of India—one provided by a multi-authored, web-based unofficial encyclopedia called Wikipedia, another by the British newspaper, *The Guardian*, and yet another by the American newspaper, *The New York Times*. Other searches with terms such as "India," "Indian history," "Indian culture," and "travel to India" would elicit similar outcomes, which would also vary with time of the search. These examples point towards a set of issues in eliciting the representation of India through the websites that might appear after a search for India on the Web.

The first issue with this representation is the difference in representations that would emerge on the computer screen based on a

---

[2] A "search engine" is a website offered by an institution that has done the computer programming needed to search through numerous websites looking for the presence of the keywords used by the user in the websites. One such popular search engine is Google provided by the Google Corporation.

Image 6.1. Website of Incredible India

Courtesy: http://incredibleindia.org/index.php/travel.

specific website which is selected by the user of the Western computer screen. If a user looks at even the first half a dozen the websites that appear higher up in the list, a set of different and contradictory representations would be visible to the audience member. Usually, users of the Web do not restrict themselves to the first website that they encounter; the very nature of the Web encourages exploration of the different digital resources that are available about a topic of interest. When the point of interest is India, and using the example cited with the search for the term "India," it would become apparent to the Western user of the computer screen that India could be any one or a combination of the following:

- An ancient country with a very large population that follows a democratic political system.[3]
- "India is the second most populous country in the world, its largest democracy and home to vast diversity in geography, climate, culture, language, and ethnicity. Its civilization predates that of Europe. India won independence from Great Britain in 1947 following protest of British rule led by Mohandas K. Gandhi. Independence split British India into India and Pakistan, resulting in continuing animosities complicated by both countries' possession of nuclear weapons."[4]

---

[3] http://en.wikipedia.org/wiki/India
[4] http://topics.nytimes.com/top/news/international/countriesandterritories/india/index.html

- A country which faces natural disaster with devastating effects, "Fresh disaster threatens with the displaced crammed into camps and bloated animal carcasses floating in stagnant water."[5]
- India is slowly developing its relations with China as reported by the *Times of India.*

These few examples begin to demonstrate the concerns with the representation of the country and its people on the computer screen. First, the representation is intimately tied to the author of the website. It is no different from the situation with the film or TV screen. There, too, the maker of the film or TV show would determine what specific strategies of representation should be used. Thus, as discussed earlier, there are variations in the image which is being produced on the traditional screens. The matter is, however, far more complex here since the representation on the computer screen has a far greater latitude of variation because the number of images is far more voluminous and the authors are widely divergent. The authors, who create a representation of India through websites themselves, subscribe to many different ideological positions and each of those ideological positions manifest itself in the image which is produced on the computer screen of the West. As a result, it is impossible for the audience to eventually arrive at a conclusion about what India is and what Indians are like. There is a regression of the meaning of "India" and in a quintessential example of the postmodern condition, the stability of a meaning seems to be called into question. India that was imagined through the traditional screens, with their relative intertextual similarity, is no longer discoverable on the computer screen, leading to a crisis of authenticity of the representation of India and Indians in the digital.

The issue of authenticity is the second concern since the authorship of the representations remains unclear on many of the websites. Other than some of the obviously recognizable international institutions, much of the representations are produced by

---

[5] http://www.theguardian.com/global-development/2014/sep/16/kashmir-serious-disease-devastating-floods-india-pakistan

authors who would be unknown to the potential audience. Indeed, the viewers of the Western screen might not even note who the authors are. The technological brilliance shown with the "bells and whistles" of a well-designed website could draw attention away from the author of the website. This issue is true for many different kinds of digital images and becomes especially important for the representation of a country and its people. Authors with different motives and experiences would encode their websites in a manner that would only represent the specific author's representation but when circulated as a mass-mediated message, such individualized representations take on an authenticity that the voice would never be able to attain through the traditional means of representation. This issue of authenticity becomes even more important as large portions of the users of the Western computer screen are the youngsters who are "digital natives," for whom worldviews are shaped by what they encounter on the computer screen. The youngsters of 2014, those who are in the ages of 10 to 15 years, often consider the information available through the Internet to be authentic. The image of India that they encounter when they Google "India" becomes the authentic image of India and the Indians.

Yet, the two issues—the multiplicity of representations and the unverified authenticity—create an internal tension over representation. Simply speaking, the user of the computer screen has to answer the fundamental question—who can be trusted? The "safety" of the movie screen and the TV screen where that media offered a screened and filtered image becomes much of "messy" when the computer screen comes into play. Eventually, when considering the websites that show up on the screen at the end of a search or by traversing from one website to another, it is clear that there are numerous sites that create a representation of India. There is no consistency in the representation, and a confusing image is produced primarily because of the lack of interaction with the author of the representation. However, there is also a class of websites where the computer screen becomes a conduit for connecting with a real individual from India in real time. These screens add another level of complexity to settling on the representation of India and its people on the computer screen since the author actually comes "alive" on the computer screen and the audience of the screen is able to interact with the Indian on the screen.

THE INDIAN ON THE SCREEN

One of the ways in which the computer screen becomes different from all the other kinds of screens is in the fact that this screen is not a passive device that only brings images and information to the viewer, but has become increasingly the site where it is possible to interact with the screen and what appears on it. Returning to the original analogy of the screen as a filter that brings only what we want to see needs to be updated and reconsidered with the computer screen because of the interactive nature of the screen. Since this screen can be customized by the user and it is possible to indicate exactly what information the user wants to see, it is also possible to fine tune the filtering effect to a point that the screen is completely opaque to anything outside what the viewer wants. Staring at such a computer screen is unlike sitting in a screened porch that keeps out the mosquitoes while offering a chance glance at a blue bird on the pine tree branch. The computer screen shuts out everything other than what the viewer wants. That bluebird will never be seen because the computer screen filters it out, based on the instructions offered by the user of the screen. In this restricted view of the world that the computer screen can potentially provide, the user does have the opportunity to delve deep into the world that the person is interested in. The breadth of ideas offered by a limited filter is replaced by the depth of ideas that can be discovered with a powerful viewing tool focused on a small set of ideas. This depth includes the possibility of interaction with people who might never have been a part of the experience without the computer screen offering the opportunities of exploring an idea deeply without the distraction of a peripheral view. Eventually, the computer screen becomes the focus as an Indian appears in "real" life on the screen. This level of focus has been made possible as Indians in India are beginning to use the computer screen as an interactive tool to offer services to the users of the screen in the West.

These interactions are often in the realm of hiring services that are more efficiently obtained from India, as has been the trend with the process of outsourcing. Briefly, the process of outsourcing involves sending a portion of a business activity to a different country. This trend has been around for a variety of institutions over a long period of time. After the advances in digital technologies, a large amount of a variety of processes has been sent to India. For a customer in the United States, the outcome of outsourcing is the direct interaction with a service agent outside the US. For instance, if there might be a problem with a bank account of a customer in America, the customer could dial an American phone number to resolve the problem and would get connected with a service agent in India who would attempt to resolve the issue. The primary motivation for outsourcing is the reduction of cost of providing service for the corporation. Since labor in India is both skilled and less expensive, the process of outsourcing is a lucrative option for international corporations. However, as an unintended outcome, the process also results in direct contact between a Western customer and an Indian service provider. Usually, this contact happens over the telephone and does not require a computer screen. With time, however, there is a growth of services where the American consumer might actually contact an Indian service provider through the computer screen using video-enabled communication systems. In this situation, the viewer of the screen has the opportunity to develop specific images of the Indian as well as the country where the person is located.

The tools required for this interaction has become commonplace—a connection to the Internet that allows data to flow fast (broadband connection), a computer program that activates the built-in camera of the computer, and two people are connected "face to face" to interact with each other. Consider, for instance, the information provided by an online tutoring system that states: "Our lesson space lets you use video, audio or text. Upload any assignment and work through it together."[6] For this particular company, the tutors are globally distributed with a majority of the tutors being located in India. In a similar fashion, there are other companies and sometimes individuals, who would

---

[6] https://instaedu.com/online-now/instaedu/?gclid=CjwKEAjwwdOhBRCG0fPrlfO1gGUS
JAC1FmHXl9b28Z0aDGItB60l9t5RWkzHv9wMpQJ2LlsxxHJC3xoCZHTw_wcB#

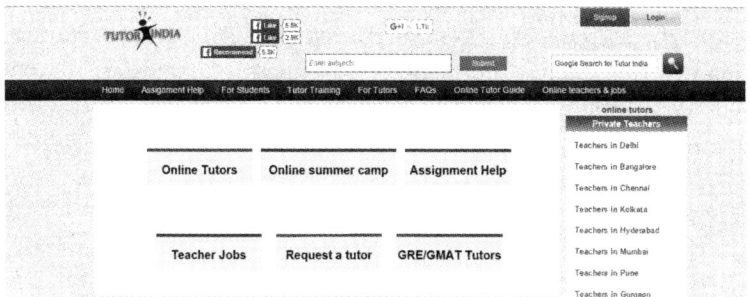

Image 6.2. Website of Online Tutorial

Courtesy: http://tutorindia.net/

use the Internet to distribute their advertisements inviting the Western audience to connect with them, to get help with academic work. A popular company that offers video phone services using the computer has developed a complete corporate division, which is focused on using the video services to bring teachers from different parts of the world, including India, into the classroom of the West using the interactive computer screen. The service which is being called "Skype in the Classroom" is still aimed at the use of the technology to offer opportunities for students in the classroom, but this trend to bring an Indian teacher to the Western audience through the computer screen is a growing tendency and a growing industry given the cost differential and efficiency gain in bringing the Indian tutor in contact with the Western student. Several popular reports are starting to pay attention to this phenomenon, as illustrated below:

> At the end of every school day, eighth-grader Taylor Robison heads home for a session with her tutor. But Taylor's tutor, Gary Ishwar, doesn't come to her house. In fact, he's never been to America. Ishwar lives in Bangalore, India—9,000 miles from Taylor's Modesto, Calif., home. A former schoolteacher who says he holds two master's degrees, Ishwar is one of a growing number of highly educated Indians now tutoring U.S. students over the Internet.[7]

---

[7] http://abcnews.go.com/WNT/Technology/story?id=2641669&page=1

"It's a 3D shape." "Wait, I'm not sure if that's a square." "Oh, I know, it's a rectangular prism, a pyramid." "Is it a cuboid?"

These are snippets of overheard conversations in a classroom at Ashmount Primary School in north London, as Year 6 pupils don headphones and study shapes with their maths tutors in India.

The pupils have been using an online one-to-one tutoring scheme—organised by a British entrepreneur—which links them to tutors more than 4,000 miles away in the city of Ludhiana in India.[8]

Kenneth Tham, a high school sophomore in Arcadia, Calif., strives to improve his grades and scores on standardized tests. Most afternoons, he is tutored remotely by an instructor speaking to him on a voice-over-Internet headset while he sits at his personal computer going over lessons on the screen. The tutor is in India.[9]

As these reports from American Broadcasting Company (ABC), BBC, and *The New York Times* demonstrate, it is a trend in the West that is steadily on the rise, where the computer screen could become the conduit to connect an individual in the West to an individual in India. The consequences could be quite provocative, given what I have discussed in this book so far where India and Indians appear as exoticized and somewhat abnormal based on the conventions of the West. In the interactions such as tutoring and other relational moments, the Indian can no longer be a spectacle of the Western gaze and the person who needs to be rescued and uplifted from her primitive condition, but the Indian is now the person who "rescuing" through the computer screen. It is the Indian tutor who now rescues a student from the horror of failing grades in high-school trigonometry and to pass the course with good grades. Most of the power relationships that were inscribed in the imaging of the Indian and India through the static screens are called into question with the interactive screen of the computer.

The power relationships change because of the change in the agency of who gets to tell the story of India. The narrative of the static screen was controlled often by authors who were in a

---

[8] http://www.bbc.com/news/education-11452881
[9] http://www.nytimes.com/2007/10/31/business/worldbusiness/31butler.html?pagewanted=all&_r=0

position of power, where they could take charge of the representational symbols, and maintain a certain formulaic standardization where the represented had little agency in terms of how they were being represented. The images of Indians and India were determined and circulated by the Western author. This is nothing novel, and much has been written and discussed about this phenomenon as in the work of authors such as Edward Said[10] who gave this phenomenon a name—orientalism in the 1978 book *Orientalism*. The terms suggested that the powerful West systematically and historically represented the "Orient" or the East in the manner the West deemed appropriate. Although, the term was used to describe the representation of Arabs the concept has been applied to other parts of the colonized East as well, as shown in the works of Homi Bhabha[11] and Gayatri Chakravorty Spivak.[12] Indeed, the notion of "hybridity" that Bhabha offers is concerned with the ways in which the postcolonial representations still rely on a hybrid culture that retains important elements of the traditional colonial representations. It was also assumed that the Oriental, in this case the Indian, had no way of directly challenging the representation. The process changes with the interactive screen where, for instance, the tutor on the screen takes on the role of an agent in an interaction where the Western audience is guided and tutored by an Indian individual. And the Western is supported and aided by a person from the country which has historically and consistently been described as an exotic and strange land. To suddenly be confronted with a tutor from that space who understands the intricacies of trigonometry or can explain the grammatical parsing of a sentence in English, offers a point of departure from the Orientalized images of the other screens discussed so far. The Indian is automatically and already placed in a position of power, in spite of the differences in English pronunciation and other markers that were once the points of exotification which have been carefully constructed and circulated on the other screens.

---

[10] Edward Said, *Orientalism*.
[11] Homi Bhabha, *The Location of Culture* (New York: Routledge Classics, 1994).
[12] Gayatri Spivak, *Can the Subaltern Speak?* 271–313.

Both in terms of the static screen of an Indian website and the dynamism of being able to speak to an Indian tutor or other service providers with the use of the computer screen begins to offer an alternative to the images that have been offered by other screens. It is an important point of inflection in the representation of the Indian on the Western screen because the representational process is moved away from an institution such as CNN to the individual such as a tutor or a friend on digital social media. The next section considers the way in which social media, such as Facebook and Orkut, also brings a different image of India and Indians on the computer screen when the digital tools bring forth the social media Indian on the computer screen.

DIGITALLY MEDIATED SOCIAL INDIAN

One of the most significant consequences of the development of digital technologies in the early twenty-first century is the rapid proliferation of the use of digital tools to make interpersonal connections. By 2014, at the time of writing this book, these tools have been adopted by millions of people, and one of the most popular such tools—Facebook—would claim to have nearly 1,300 million users, which makes it one of the largest collection of people in one single digital space. One of the characteristics of this place is the fact that the place has no geographic definition and no geographic boundaries. Spaces such as Facebook are populated by people who could be anywhere in the world, and their representation is produced by the digital presence which comes through the computer screen. These presences are carefully crafted profiles that offer an image of an individual, and other individuals interacting with him/her through the computer are able to befriend the digital profile and establish a connection with the individual who is represented on the computer screen. Through this process, the individuals offering these profiles are able to interact with each other independent of where they live or what nationality they have.

Also, in 2014, the number of active users of the digital social media system, Facebook, in India surpassed 100 million, whereas in North America the number of active users was 204 million at the same time. Other parts of the West also had a significant number of Facebook users. For a moment, using the example of Facebook, it is quite likely that a Western user of Facebook, interacting with the system through the computer screen, could well be interacting with the profile of a person of Indian origin. In the increasingly interconnected world where people from different nations and places are made to congregate at a university, a workplace, or a physical neighborhood, there are increasingly more connections between people. In these cases, one individual might not have any real life connection with another individual but are connected digitally through social media "seeing" each other on the computer screen.

The way the system of digital social media is organized, it is not uncommon to have connections that are made possible only because of the technology. Consider, for instance, a situation where a person from India works in a multinational corporation. It is quite likely that in addition to the multitude of digital social media "friends" who are from India, this person could also have a set of "friends" who the person has befriended through professional connections. This person is now the conduit through which friends can interact with each other—people who could belong to different cultures and different spaces. This interaction could take on many different forms. Continuing with the example, it is possible that the connector creates a visual narb[13] with a photograph of an Indian celebration such as Diwali—the Indian festival of lights and the Indian new year (for some communities)—and the narb would show up on the computer screen of the Western friend. In that moment, an image of India has been created that is different from anything that many of the other screens could produce—it is a personal image of a person who is not a stranger, but a friend, albeit from India.

The potential of digital social media lies in personalizing the image where the image of oil lamps of Diwali is no different from the pictures of a Bar Mitzvah—the Jewish coming of age ceremony for boys—or the images of a Thanksgiving turkey dinner of an American family. This personalization commences with the digital interactive services such as tutoring and other similar one-on-one

---

[13] A narb is the short form for the term "narrative bit," which refers to a small piece of information that an individual can produce and circulate on a social media site. A narb could be a status update, a picture, or a video that the individual makes available on a social media site such as Facebook.

real-time interactions, but digital social media explodes that to a different level because of the volume of people who populate the digital space and immense possibilities of interaction between the people. The potential of this interaction is best demonstrated with a small example. Since 2009, President Barak Obama has been holding a Diwali celebration at the White House. Setting aside the debates over the reasons for doing this, it is also the case that a video recording of the short speech by the President often finds it way on to digital social media where a person, often of Indian origin, would place the video online. One of my Facebook friends of Indian origin created a video narb with the video of the President. Thereafter, it becomes interesting when my friend's friends began to approve the video by "liking" it and/or by commenting on it. In another case, in 2014, one of the comments came from a non-Indian person, which was then followed by an interaction between several non-Indian friends of my friend. In that instant, an image of India was being created where the users of the Western screen were able to talk to each other to recreate the image of India and Indians. The institutional images of the movie and TV screen begin to get replaced by the individual voices of the people from India and of Indian origin, who take the shape of the "real" people and not just the generic image demanded by the Western institutional image merchants. Digital social media offers the opportunity for individual social connections through the computer screen where the metaphor of "friend" becomes immensely provocative and powerful.

Never before in the history of creating the image of relationship between Indians and the West was emphasized by "friend"ship. Digital social media added this layer to the process of creating an image on the Western computer screen. India was no longer a distant place with distant and different people. India was now right on the screen made alive by real people who are friends of friends. The barriers of distance and time to create friendships were partly removed as the computer screen streamed in profile pictures and home videos of celebration of events ranging from the Indian Diwali festival to the personal birthday celebration at home. These images on the computer screen did not offer a narrative of difference, but a narrative of similarity, a narrative that showed Indian homes adorned with oil lamps for Diwali and Christmas trees for Christmas. Most importantly, the images on the computer screen called into question the other images created by other screens. Also, it created an image that is multifaceted, sometimes internally contradictory, and most importantly, this image was not monolithic and focused, but a composite of many images.

THE COMPOSITE IMAGE ON THE COMPUTER SCREEN

The changes in technology have opened up some unique possibilities in representing people and places as pointed out here. This new screen is not as much a filter and barrier; on the contrary, it is a screen with an open-ended potential where the images become much less controlled and institutionally manufactured as in the case of the traditional media. This departure creates a crisis in the representation since it creates an internally contradictory and composite image that no longer subscribes to the conventional and "natural" image of India and Indians. I would argue that the principal reason for this difference lies in the fact that these images are produced through the voices and discourses of people who do not have to subscribe to any specific ideologically "acceptable" and familiar set of representational practices. India and Indians on the computer screen do not have to appear exotic or different, and if they do, it is because a specific individual chooses that option just as another individual could choose a different option. This diversity of images is the direct result of the empowering of a multitude of voices that help to compose the image.

It is, therefore, useful to consider the importance of the notion of "voice" in this discussion. The notion of "voice" has been particularly important in thinking about the way in which new digital technologies have offered opportunities for many to create their own point of view regarding any matter that might not have "coverage" on the institutional media. For instance, in the late-1990s, I had the opportunity to examine the way in which South Asian women were using the Web to create an image of themselves with the discourses that they produced and thus were able to present their own representation of self. There are many examples of such moments that demonstrate that the computer screen becomes the conduit of opening up a new and different world of images, performing much less like the sieve that the other screens do. This ability to have many voices also creates conditions where the viewer has to sift through the different representations to eventually create the composite representation which could have contradictory elements within itself. For instance, a website might focus on the poverty in India whereas another could highlight the mansion of a rich industrialist of India. It is the viewer who has to decide what the authentic India is even if it is difficult to find an authentic India or Indian, especially when India and Indians have so many different elements that define and describe the entities.

It is all these different and diverse elements that combine in a composite image on the computer screen. There is no longer a specific and "real" India that was filtered in by the other screens but it is now a heteroglossic India where the many (hetero) tongues (glossa) speak together to offer a representation, and not any single voice can claim authority on an image brought forth on the computer screen.[14] This is the new India which is emerging in the digital space, accessible to anyone with access to a computer and a connection to the Internet. The audience of this screen is, thus, not restricted to the Western audience but to anyone, including people of Indian origin, who is interested in understanding India and the people of that land. However, among this audience, the ones of Indian origin are of special interest since this audience is also shifting and changing as discussed in the earlier chapter about immigration and diaspora. There is an increasingly large Indian audience in the West which is also accessing the screens discussed so far to imagine India through these filters. Many in this audience might not have any experience of being in the physical space of India, but are connected to the nation and its people by genetic origins and a screen in addition to the ones discussed so far—the satellite screen. The next chapter explores the ways in which the satellite technology is also bringing images of India on the Western screens, albeit for a specific audience of people who claim some past connection with India.

---

[14] The notion of heteroglossia was suggested by the Russian linguist Mikhail Bakhtin in his 1934 article Слово в романе [Slovo v romane], published in English as "Discourse in the Novel."

7. THE SATELLITE SCREEN

S atellite technology for the transmission of images to the TV screen has been around from the early 1980s, and it was used by commercial TV networks, such as CNN, to send their programs to TV screens by tying up with cable TV companies. These cable companies would use the commercial grade satellite reception material, often called the satellite dish, to pluck the signals off the satellites and then send them over cable to the customers who have paid and subscribed for the cable service. This model of distributing images to TV screens is what has been discussed earlier in this book. However, starting in the early-2000s, another model of distributing images came into play where a private individual could obtain a satellite dish, then work with a satellite distribution company and point the dish at the appropriate satellite for obtaining the images on the TV screen. This form of distribution led to the development of satellite TV where small dishes mushroomed across the Western landscape and then globally, as images from traditional distributors were supplemented by images received

Image 7.1. Watching Satellite Distribution of Indian Programs at an American Home

Courtesy: Author.

from the satellite. A brief review of the tools for satellite distribution would help reveal how this new tool impacts the images of Indian on the Western screen, especially for a small, but important segment of the Western audience.

SATELLITE TECHNOLOGY

The tools required to receive a signal from a satellite is merely a small metal dish which can be placed in a way that the dish has an unobstructed view of the satellite in space. After that, the dish connects to a device that interprets the signals picked up from the satellite and makes them visible on the screen. The interpreting device is often called the satellite box. In the United States, there are two major corporations which provide the dish and the box and the subscriber has to work with the service provider to set up the dish and the box. The actual signal reaching the satellite could come from a variety of different sources—from the Western corporation who dominate the media landscape to other less prominent global and ethnic sources. It is a fact that the satellite in the sky can be the point of broadcast for signals from a variety of sources that makes this tool especially interesting for this analysis. A TV screen located in Winston-Salem in the state of North Carolina in the US, when connected to a satellite box and dish, can receive the same signals that a TV screen located at Raigarh in the state of Chhattisgarh, when connected to a satellite box and dish, can receive. Much like the way in which the Internet technology makes content globally available, so does the satellite technology, with the difference being the fact that the images obtained from the satellite is usually viewed on the traditional TV screens.

Most companies offering satellite TV technology offer different kinds of programs that the users can subscribe to. Given the global reach of the technology, it is possible for users to subscribe to content that could have emanated from a completely different part of the world than where the audience is located. Thus, the corporations in the USA offer India Packages on their satellite networks and a subscriber in New York could choose to subscribe to channels from the major distributors of TV content in India. For instance, at home in the US, my family has access to nearly 25 major Indian channels. And it is as simple as a press of a button on a remote control device to switch from the live telecast of the basketball game between Wake Forest University and a rival college to the live telecast of a cricket one-day international match between India and England. This technology thus becomes particularly attractive to a portion of the audience in the West who yearn for the connection with the media of India, especially as a way to remain connected with the culture of the place of origin when the audience experiences the diasporic condition. This connection is built around and based upon the images that are offered on the screen by the satellite signal.

THE IMAGES

These images are built around a variety of program genres that have proliferated over time. It is useful to examine the vast array of program categories that produce these images for the diasporic in the United States. Other countries have slight variations of the categories found in the USA. A useful starting point of this exploration is to consider the variety of programs that the major satellite signal providers offer in the USA.

There are two major satellite service providers in the USA who cover a majority of the areas where the diasporic Indians' cluster is in the USA. Both the providers offer standard American television programming and international programming that can be purchased for a price. These programs are offered in different tiers where the customer can choose from a set of genres of programs as well from different languages used in India. The selection of genre is often dependent on specific television channels that are popular in India. It is useful to consider the television industry in India at this point. In India, much of television programming is offered by a set of commercial channels, which are already built upon the satellite network. India was one of the countries that adopted the satellite technology very early in the development of the satellite-based television transmission. Over nearly three decades, with the changes in the Indian economy, the media space in India has been populated by numerous national and international satellite-based channels that have become far more popular than the state-owned television production and distribution system. The private corporations operating in India are led by multinational groups, such as Sony Corporation and Sky Corporation, which have developed programs specially designed for the Indian market. It is these same channels that become available in the USA. Thus, a person could be watching the range of programs offered by the Sony channels in India as well as in the USA. All these channels offer a range of programming which includes all major television program genres—soap operas, news, comedy, sports, and religious programs. Consider, for instance, the programs offered in the USA by one of the leading satellite services. On their web page for South Asian programs, they first offer programs in 10 different languages. Within these 10 languages, the greatest amount of choice is offered in Hindi where, in 2015, the customer can choose from 12 different bundles of programs with the most expensive bundle being $55 per month. However, this sum of money opens up a whole new world on the screen for the customer. For this price, the customer would gain access to 36 channels of Indian programs that would be brought by the satellite to the Western screen in the home of the diasporic Indian. These channels include all the major satellite program providers operating in India, namely, TV Today, Viacom TV group offering the Colors channels such as Aapka Colors, the Indian steel magnate Lakshmi Mittal's B4U range of channels, MTV, Prannoy Roy's NDTV, the Indian version of CNN, India-based Sahara channels, Sony channels, Asia Star broadcastings TV Asia, Zee channels, Times Now a news channel offered by the Times Group in India, and continuous cricket on Willow TV which is offered by an American precisely for the diasporic communities across the world interested in cricket. As noted earlier, it is also possible for the viewer to obtain programs, again at a small cost, in the regional language of the audience.

These numerous channels offer continuous programs that offer a large range of options to the viewers. A fair amount of the programming is based on the material from Bollywood, the massive movie industry of India. Several channels dedicate their entire programming to the distribution of new and old Bollywood movies. The satellite channels in regional languages of India also have its share of movies from the regional film industry. Bollywood and regional movie industries are also featured through the satellite channels that bring continuous music videos from Bollywood to the Western screen. There are various channels, such as Zoom, which focus entirely on music videos. The Indian film industry offers a unique art form where nearly every film has a set of song and dance sequences which becomes "stand-alone" music videos that are broadcasted continuously by many satellite broadcasters. Finally, there is a spin-off set of programs that deal with Bollywood and its stars, scandals and gossips. For instance, STAR network's *Koffee with Karan* has proved to be an immensely popular program on the Western screen where a noted Bollywood personality—Karan Johar—would have a conversation with other Bollywood personalities.

The second major category of programs is that of related to news and events. Much like Western television, the Indian news broadcast industry has also adopted a nonstop news format, sometimes in collaboration with Western news behemoths such as Cable News Network (CNN). The indigenous news channels have also become very sophisticated in their program variety and have gained the ability to quickly "break" news while broadcasting live events globally. For instance, viewers in the West were able to watch the historic Republic Day parade of 2015 when the Indian prime minister and the American president presided over the parade in New Delhi. Now, the viewer of the Western screen can watch such events without having to wait for it to show up on the Western TV systems. As an addendum to the news program category, it is important to note that there has also been a growth in talk show programs that are available on the Western screen connected to a satellite broadcast system. This category of programs has produced talk show hosts such as Arnab Goswami who has become infamous for his abrasive style of doing interviews. These programs have also entered Western homes via satellite.

Finally and perhaps most importantly, the entire category of programs can generally be called "soap operas." As I had noted in my book[1] in 1986, the soap opera was an emergent program category three decades ago but even then, as it is now, the Indian soap opera is different from the Western version because of the subcategories that belong within the soap opera format. For instance, there are soap operas that could be called religious soap operas that are based often on Hindu mythologies and gods and goddesses. Additionally, there are socially relevant programming that looks like soap operas or miniseries that deal with relevant social issues in India, such as *Satyamev Jayate* program produced by Amir Khan—a notable Indian actor. This program addresses social issues on "reality TV" and "soap opera" style to discuss the pressing social issues of the country. While these program categories are important, the largest category of soap operas are the ones that are like traditional soap operas which narrate expansive and dramatic stories of families much like the soap operas of the West. However, Indian programmers were quick to adopt a uniquely Indian look for these soap operas which were usually called "serials" in the Indian nomenclature. For instance, the regime of serials on Indian television took on a curious and specific style with the appearance of auteurs such as Ekta Kapoor. Growing up on the movies of Bollywood, such serial makers were able to capture some of the key emotions of the Indian population in India and produce such popular shows that focused on relationships between family members all living under the same roof. In many cases, these homes and locations would be lavishly decorated and furnished and the protagonists would be presented in a superlatively dressed and bejeweled fashion. Much like serials

---

[1] Anand Mitra, 1986.

and soap operas from all places, the shows made by the people such as Ekta Kapoor presented an imaginary India that looked excellent on the TV screen and dealt with issues that are close to Indians, albeit in a manner that was visually attractive. Although these serials had an "unreal" look, for instance, few homes of the viewing audience would be as lavish as the ones in these programs, this category of programs became immensely popular.

The image of India is, thus, built around these major categories of programs that are beamed on the Western screens of the diasporic Indians living all over the world. To this audience, these images on the screen could be the only connection with a land that they have left many years before and did not have an opportunity to return to. To some others in the diaspora, it is a land of their parents and grandparents, and a land that they have an affinity with but which they will never be able to visit. To all these audiences, which are a growing number, India is imaged through the programs that are available through the satellite broadcasts.

INDIA FOR INDIANS IN DIASPORA

As I have pointed out earlier in the book, the notion of an Indian in diaspora has become increasingly complex with time since many different people, just in the USA, falling into this category and the matter gets even more convoluted when considering people who are not in the USA but still a part of the diaspora. Scholars have considered the issue of Indians in the diaspora with great diligence—from important academic research to popular novels—and there is little agreement about the way to understand and analyze this vast diaspora. For the current project, I am considering the diaspora from the perspective of the audience of the satellite-mediated message brought to the Western screen. As in the case of critical audience analysis, it becomes useful to consider how this unique audience would decode the images on the screen and then gain an understanding of the people and place the image represents. What is unique about this section of the book is that it purposefully focuses on the Indian audience as opposed to the more generalized Western audience. Yet, this Indian audience is of paramount importance because ultimately it is these people in the diaspora who are the most vulnerable to the way in which India is represented on all the Western screens discussed so far. The Indian programs on satellite are not viewed by the Western audience, so they have a specific Western look at India, but the Indian audience in the West is simultaneously watching the Western depiction of India and the "authentic" depiction of India through the satellite screen. To unravel this, I would suggest that we have to assume a few aspects of the audience, especially in terms of their cultural proximity to India, to understand and decode the images that are depicted on the screen.

At the time of writing this book in 2014–15, it was known that the Indian-American community in the USA is made up of many different types of people. A simple way to categorize the people would be to consider their place of birth and the time they have spent away from India. First, there are those who were born in India and have between 30 to 50 years away from India, having built their lives in the USA from an early age of the mid-twenties when they arrived in the USA as a portion of the classic "brain drain" of the 1960s after the USA opened its borders to people from India among other countries in Asia. Next, there is a second group who were also born in India and have spent anywhere between 3 to 30 years in the USA, and have little desires to return to India and plan to live the rest of their lives in the USA. There is another group of people who were also born in India and have been in the USA for less than three years, who either will return to India or are undecided about their future location. The next set of the audience are not born in India and are Americans ranging from the youngsters being born now to those who are in the 45–55 age group. This last group often has little connection with India as a country but is in close proximity to the people who were born in India. For instance, my son of 20-years age was born in the USA but has grown up with us (me and my wife) who were born in India and have lived in the USA for nearly 35 years. Our son has thus been heavily exposed to the images of India as shown in the satellite broadcasts. It is this audience that watches the broadcasts from India and based on their category and their frequency of travel to India, they decode the images differently creating images of India in their minds that are quite unique.

The issue of frequency of travel is quite important as well. For instance, even though I have been in the USA for nearly 35 years, I have travelled to India nearly a 100 times in that time span. On the other hand, I know of people who have left India for 10 years but have never travelled back to their native land. The sojourn to India for this audience is also an important factor in the way the image is produced. Generally, the frequency of travel has gone up with time, but there are many diasporic Indians, both born in India and born outside India, who would claim that they are never able to go back to India for long periods of time for a variety of reasons. The combination of the place of birth, the length of time outside India, and the frequency of visits to India creates different kinds of audiences who could image India in many different ways based on the images brought to the Western screen by satellite.

Those who are familiar with India would see the reflection of a contemporary urban India in many of the programs that are popular. The news shows, the Bollywood-based shows, sports and some of the serials depict the India that is moving toward an important place in the global finance and politics. For instance, the Republic Day parades of 2015 would appear quite "real" to the diasporic audience who is familiar with the way India looks today, in terms of its development and status in the world. This is the audience which would also see the ways in which some programs, such as the social serials, appear to exaggerate the real India with a lavishness that is not reflective of the majority of India. Soap operas and such serials have been known to do this for any culture the programs depict. Much has been written about the ways in which American soap operas are far from the reality of the average American life, and the average American viewer knows well that there is a large distance between the "reality" of American life and the images that are produced by soap operas. This understanding of the difference is most likely within the diasporic who have maintained a sense of connection with India and what happens there. For the diasporic who have been disconnected from India, the programs could get baffling and create a peculiar idea of India which nevertheless remains the country of their origin or the country of the origin of their parents and grandparents, even if the parents and grandparents are also diasporic.

To such audiences, India would appear as a place that is simultaneously hyper-Westernized. It is happening with many of the programs depicting an Americanized India that is also somewhat culturally liberal as depicted in many of the music programs and

Image 7.2. Satellite Dishes at an Indian-American Home in the USA

Courtesy: Author.

Bollywood-based programs. It is also evident from the "item songs" of Bollywood that could surpass the sexual innuendos of many Western music videos, and from the members participating in talk shows and interviews who would openly appear Western and freely speak of the issues that would be or have been a taboo sometimes ago. To the diasporic audience, it is an alien India, especially if their memories go back 10, 15, or 20 years in the past. The modern India, seen on the Western screen of the diasporic homes with satellite dishes, is certainly not the India they left behind. On the other hand, for those who have never been to India but have a diasporic connection, it is an India that looks more like the West than what they have been led to believe by their diasporic families or by the depiction seen on the many other screens discussed earlier in the book. It is no longer the India of elephants and snake-charmers that still show up on many of the screens I discussed earlier. On the contrary, it is an India where TV talk show hosts scream at their guests in much the same way that many do in talk shows of the West. The India seen through Indian TV programs is a place where young men and women dress exactly as the one's do in the West, and they interact almost exactly as they do in the West. For the diasporic, this is a new India—one that is rapidly westernizing and developing in a manner they either do not remember or have never been told about.

At the same time, the images present another India, deeply rooted in the India that the diasporic left behind. Some of the material available to the diasporic viewer is very reminiscent of an India that is steeped in tradition and primarily Hindu ideology and customs. Consider, for instance, elements such as Prem Jyotish, an astrological service that continues to advertise its astrological ware to the diasporic Indian who could be in need of that support in the foreign land. There are also several other categories of programs that deal with religious themes including regular prayer sessions and sermons, very similar to the Christian Evangelical programming that is seen on Western, especially American, television on Sunday mornings. The programs about Hindu religion and a Hindu way of life could actually offer a moment of solace for those in the diaspora who seek that connection with the land they left behind and for those in the diaspora who might have never seen that land. For the later, these programs become a way of reminding them of the land of their parents and grandparents. The proverbial "traditional India" shows up in other forms of programs as well, including some of the soap operas and serials where traditional themes related to family and relationships are discussed in the narratives that would focus on issues such as arranged marriages, dowry, and other controversial issues that Indians in India are grappling with, but to the diasporic with minimal contact, these becomes indicators that they can identify with.

The image that is produced, therefore, has internal contradictions which make full sense when one considers the primary audience of these programs that are beamed on the Western screen through satellite dishes. These are meant for Indians in India who are immersed within the culture that is being depicted on the Indian screen in Indian homes. Thus, the mothers-in-law and the daughters-in-law who watch the serials sitting in Kanpur in India might not dress in quite the same way or might not live in similar mansions, but could share a certain resonance with the themes of the narratives.[2] For the diasporic, it presents a confusing image where the "real" India is lost in all the contradictory narratives and representations. On one hand, a social activist television program might

---

[2] http://timesofindia.indiatimes.com/nri/contributors/contributions/deepa-duraisamy/Saas-bahus-and-beyond-Indian-television/articleshow/13031090.cms

revolt against entrenched social practices related to gender and race, but the same issues are treated in a different way in a serial. These contradictions are true for most of the television systems across the Globe. Indeed, these contradictions should be expected and encouraged in the free market of ideas, so that the audience has a choice and can make informed decisions. The curious aspect of this process, with respect to the satellite image on the Western screen, is that the viewing audience has no specific decision to make and they do not even have familiarity with the place that is being depicted or the practices being critiqued. As a result, the image simply acts as a way to imagine a place which is foreign but nostalgically intimate. It is a unique situation that has scarcely happened before where those in diaspora are drawn back to an imaginary place of origin through the mediated images that enter their Western screen from their place of origin.

Yet, it is this place that has been shown on many of the Western screens in many different ways. The diasporic live in the same geographic space where the Western screen has the most influence. For the diasporic, it is an important phenomenon because the diasporic are the ones who feel the most important effects of the way in which India and Indians are imaged on the Western screen. While most people in the West are not familiar with the television programs from India brought to the West by satellite, the people in the West who are watching the images of India and Indians on the Western screen see around them the diasporic. To a casual observer in the West, the diasporic are simply Indian—people do not hold a sign declaring their number of years in the West or their citizenship. In the view of the Western audience, the person from India is often conflated with the images that have appeared on the Western screen. For the diasporic, the interaction with the world around them is complicated by the fact that they are attributed the characteristics based on the screen image, while the diasporic person might also be only aware of India through the same images that the attributor makes or through the same images supplemented by the images discussed in this chapter.

Eventually, the culmination of the images happen in three spheres of interaction—between the Indian in the West and the Western, between the Indian in India and the Western in India, and between the Indian in the West and the Indian in India. The next section of the book focuses on these three aspects.

8. THE INDIAN IN THE WEST

Much of the media research has focused on the project of content analysis to extract specific themes from the different forms of representation that are available in various media spaces. To a large extent, that has been the project of this book as well. As pointed out in the previous chapters, there are many different ways in which India and Indians are presented on the Western screen. These presentations are meant for different segments of audiences and, therefore, bring forth different kinds of images that would be most popular or familiar to the specific audiences targeted. The fact that the different audiences will read different images in different ways requires that the images be constructed in different ways. Consequently, these images would often contradict each other when compared. For instance, as discussed in the previous chapters, while the computer screen might have images of a modern India with a strong Western influence, the India on the Western TV screen might offer the images of a backward country with terrible issues with safety for rural women. The

Image 8.1. Indian-American Artist Performing at an India Festival in the USA

Courtesy: Author.

authentic India might never be found in the collage of images that are paraded on the Western screen. Perhaps, it is also futile to seek the "authentic" since that presumes the existence of a quintessential and uncontested India. That rarely happens for a place which is as vast as India, with the amount of internal diversity and contradictions it possesses. Something more important to see is what aspects of India have been privileged on the different Western screens. That has been the goal of this project thus far—demonstrating the ways in which the representations have offered specific images by choosing particular things to focus on circulating, especially when considering the institutional media such as film and television.

While the process of finding the images remains within the realm of critical analysis of the available content, another part of any media-centric project is to ask the "so what" question; where it is important to question the significance of the findings from the analysis of the contempt. One aspect of the significance lies in the ways these images might have had an impact on one or more sets of audiences in the West.

There are many different ways of going about answering that question depending on specific approaches to social sciences and the different ways of conceptualizing the notion of the audience. Large numbers of studies have looked at the "effect" of mediated images by quantitatively measuring the attitudes and behaviors of the people who have been exposed to the messages. In such approaches, the audience is often considered to be a large and homogeneous group who feel the effects of media and react to it in a way that can easily be measured. For instance, political pollsters spend significant time and energy in understanding the effects of political messages by measuring the reactions of the target and test audiences. Other researchers, who are often skeptic of the "quantification" of human emotions, prefer a more descriptive approach to measure effects by engaging small numbers of the audience in detailed conversations about the messages. Drawing upon the anthropological tradition of ethnographic research,[1] this strategy is often used in conducting focus group meetings to gauge the way a message would be received by an audience. The Hollywood industry is well known for testing alternative endings of movies through conversations with test audiences to decide upon the ending that would be most appealing to the audience. Yet other researchers would observe the audience carefully to understand the ways in which the audience is interacting with the media. Such observations might happen in unobtrusive ways to simply see what the audience is "doing" with the message to get a sense of the effect of the message. The observational studies of the audience draw upon the traditions of ethnography and add the element of the analysis of the inter-text; the conversations that audiences have about the images, how they decode the images, and incorporate that meaning into their everyday lives.[2]

While such approaches offer an understanding of a specific set of messages—a political advertisement, a specific episode of a show, or a specific movie—the matter gets much more complicated when the goal is to understand the way in which a specific country and its people are viewed by others in the world. Given

---

[1] This form of research is very popular among cultural anthropologists who would spend time with target groups participating in the lives of those they study while observing the cultural practices and developing a thorough and nuanced description of what they observe. This approach was popularized in the 1970s by American anthropologist Clifford Geertz (*The Interpretation of Culture,* New York: Basic Books, 1977).

[2] This approach was popularized by British scholars David Morley and Charlotte Brundson in the 1970s and 1980s at the Center for Contemporary Cultural Studies of the University of Birmingham in their analysis of the audience of a popular British show called the "Nationwide."

Image 8.2. Audience of Different Ethnicities at an India Festival in the USA

Courtesy: Author.

Image 8.3. Stalls Selling Indian Products at an India Festival in the USA

Courtesy: Author.

the variety of the messages and the diversity of the audience, any analysis remains incomplete in its scope by either missing to look at a set of messages or ignoring an important segment of the audience. There, effects research becomes incomplete and somewhat contrived; without connection with the role, messages could play in the world where the messages take on a role that cannot simply be measured by any of the approaches suggested. Indeed, the challenge is not in understanding how specific messages affect specific audiences, but how a complete gestalt of a nation and its people is created by a variety of interconnected, yet contradictory, messages. The audience of the Western screens, discussed in this book, is not tied only to the screens discussed here but is also subjected to other forms of discourse and messages about India and Indians. The audience is also confronted with people from India, and the individuals in the audience will bring all of their knowledge and experience about India to the forefront when thinking of India. The answer to the "So what?" question is necessarily more complicated and the question itself needs to become more nuanced and needs to be transformed to "So how does the Western audience mobilize their knowledge about India and Indians, partly based on the images on the Western screens, to negotiate their interactions with India and Indians when called upon to do so?"

To answer this question, I choose an alternative approach where I examine specific real moments in the history that deal with the negotiations that are increasingly becoming commonplace in the West as the opportunities of interactions expand and the nature of the audience becomes further complicated with the emergence of different kinds of Western audiences. It is not as if the Western audience is a group that is completely different from Indians; there are moments when the Western audience itself is also Indian and, at that moment, its interactions with other Indians become even more problematic as I would demonstrate here. I would also focus primarily on America when considering the different audience categories with emphasis on the interactions that are witnessed in America. Specifically, I am interested in examining how different generations of Indians living in the West negotiate identity in the West—primarily America—and how an American negotiates identity in India when the American is in India. By looking through the specific incidences and reports, I would argue that these negotiations are informed by the way in which India and Indians have been represented on the Western screen.

It is important here to revisit the idea of "stereotypes," which is related to the discussion to follow. As discussed earlier, it is often the case that the identities attributed to a person become the basis for the way a person is treated in the public sphere. It is often what is being called "stereotype" and much of the research of stereotypes focuses on the representation, suggesting that one of the sources of stereotypes is indeed the way in which a group of people is imaged and imagined. These imaginations are used to inform a lot of aspects of everyday life—from the way in which interpersonal interactions occur to the expectations related to a specific place or space. It is possible to explore the congruence between the images that become the source of making attributions and the attributions that are made to see how they are related to each other. Naturally, with a vast canvas, such as India and Indians, there are many different types of images and imaginations, just as there are many different attributions. Here, I look at a set of cases where specific interactions happen with Indians in America that appear to resonate with the images that are available on the Western screen. Some of these moments are well known and well documented, while others are the everyday interactions that many first-generation immigrants in the Unites States have to deal with but eventually become used to.

INTERACTING WITH INDIANS

The process of diaspora has created conditions and opportunities where different generations of the diasporic Indian would be interacting with the people of the United States in many domains of everyday life. Each domain presents different conditions of interaction that is influenced by the elements of images on the Western screen.

The Workplace

The most frequent domain of interaction is the workplace where a person from India works with non-Indians. Since a great portion of Indians are employed as professionals, especially in the United States, a good amount of interaction is happening there. In certain professions, the number of people of Indian origin is quite substantial. For instance, the US Census reported in 2012 that nearly 66 percent of people of Indian origin work in managerial roles in different industries in the USA. Consequently, there are opportunities for interaction with the educated and professional population of the United States as well. In general, these interactions are constructive and polite with some layers of the recognition of the Indianness of a coworker who might have some special characteristics, reminiscent of the images seen on the screen. One of the images deal with the way people speak English in India and that has been parodied and pointed out in many different images on all the different screens as discussed earlier. This issue appears as a concern in the interactions between Indians and others at workplace. In many cases, the very fact that one looks Indian is a marker that the English and pronunciation would be different. In a blog related to the differences in the accents of people of Indian or South Asian origin, an independent filmmaker and author writes about such interactions:

> At a previous workplace, I recall the difficultly one of my Indian co-workers faced due to his accent. He was explaining a transaction to a white customer, but she grew impatient and shouted, "I can't understand you! I can't understand you!" I stepped in and explained verbatim what my co-worker said and the woman understood and thanked me. I couldn't help but notice what had just happened. My co-worker, although perfectly understandable and far more knowledgeable than me with regard to the work field, was yelled at because of the way he spoke, while I, a fellow brown man, was treated respectfully and as more "competent" because of my white suburban American accent.[3]

Such moments arise in the workplace of many people in the West, where the very fact that one knows English is called into question given the images that are displayed on the Western screen. Even though the Indian minority in the USA is often considered the "model minority" because of their contributions to the country, it is not necessarily possible to escape from the images that are presented on the screen.[4] As I suggested earlier, the interactions at the

---

[3] https://muslimreverie.wordpress.com/2012/08/24/mocking-foreign-accents-and-the-privilege-of-sounding-white/

[4] The notion of 'model minority' is fraught with contradictions and tensions, see the work of Rupam Saran published in 2007 that demonstrate how the term has been

workplace are often based on stereotypes that have been produced by the images. Consider, for example, advice offered in an article in *Diversity Inc.*, where the authors suggest a list of things not to say to coworkers from places such as India. Among these, the one that holds the first place is:

> You speak English well. Where did you learn it?
>
> Typically meant as a compliment, this is one comment that really "pushes my buttons," says Anand. "Just because a person has an accent—and possible appearance—that's different than the main-stream" results in the assumption that a person can't communicate.[5]

Numerous images on the screen have presented this aspect about the Indian and the process manifests in the workplace. The issue of English is just one of the ways in which the images become important in the workplace. Other related issues deal with the "exoticness" of being from India which ranges from the kind of clothes the Indian coworker would wear to the kind of food one warms in the communal kitchen at the workplace. There are no careful studies related to such interactions, but there are reports that show up in digital discourses and personal accounts of people of Indian origin. Consider, for instance, an article published in the Houston Press on January 19, 2010, titled, "The 5 Smelliest Foods You Should Never Bring to the Office," which lists the following:

> Maybe you don't live in an area with a high concentration of curry fans. But if you live in, say, the United Kingdom or Houston—where we have lots of curry eaters—you know the aroma of a freshly-microwaved bowl of Indian food. It's delicious...to the person eating it. To everyone else, the strong scent of the curry punches you in the face with a force that makes your eyes water and your nose run. Worse—like the burnt popcorn smell—the overwhelming

---

mobilized by the dominant systems to pitch a "race war" between minorities in the USA to delegitimize the claim that minorities in a society could need support to move forward. The model minority argument is often invoked to demonstrate how a set of minorities were able to move forward without such external help. See http://krepublishers.com/06-Special%20Volume-Journal/T-Anth-00-Special%20Volumes/Anth-SI-02-Indian%20Diaspora-Web/T-Anth-SI-02-06-067-079-Saran-R/T-Anth-SI-02-06-067-079-Saran-R-Tt.pdf

[5] http://www.diversityinc.com/things-not-to-say/7-things-not-to-say-to-asian-americans/

aroma lingers for days, making your entire workplace smell like the line cook's clothes at Bombay Brasserie after pulling a double.[6]

While this and other such reports circulating in the digital sphere might have a light-heartedness about the report, it is the case that the notion of "curry" and food choices of people from India has been a point of discussion on the screen images that represent the food in many different ways, from the disgusting unauthentic monkey brains in *Indiana Jones and the Temple of Doom* to the way in which TV shows such as *Bing Bang Theory* represent the food eaten by the Indian protagonist in the comedy show.

Similar attributions are made about the clothes that people from India, particularly women, wear in the images on the screen and the attributions that result in the workplace. Although the American laws forbid discrimination in the workplace based on attire,[7] there are informal ways in which this issue becomes important. In her book, *Becoming American, Being Indian: An Immigrant Community in New York City*, Madhulika Shankar Khandelwal[8] offers references from Indian women in the American workplace, and one of the women interviewed by the author says, "One cannot wear an Indian dress like mine in an office like mine. If you do so, your colleagues will admire you or even give you compliments, but as a result, they consider you an outsider who will never be treated equally."[9] This precisely captures the tension, because of the congruence between the images seen on the screen, that offer the "otherness" of being from India and the actual person wearing the Indian outfit seen on the screen. The natural attribution that follows is one of the separations. Even the notions of diversity and inclusion are discussed in the handbooks of the Human Resources officials; the reality of the attributions cannot be escaped within a

---

[6] http://blogs.houstonpress.com/eating/2010/01/stinky_office_foods.php

[7] http://www.eoc.sa.gov.au/eo-you/workers/work/dress-codes-workplace

[8] Madhulika S. Khandelwal, *Becoming American, Being Indian: An Immigrant Community in New York City* (Ithaca: Cornell University Press, 2002).

[9] https://books.google.com/books?id=jZsZKj0FrBgC&pg=PA45&lpg=PA45&dq=clothes+for+women+from+india+in+US+workplace&source=bl&ots=XGi_zVONgN&sig=cGBV Sd28gtUJKmQTXyxUQ58TaiQ&hl=en&sa=X&ei=Un78VKeNKIixggT2r4OoCQ&ved=0 CEMQ6AEwAg#v=onepage&q=clothes%20for%20women%20from%20india%20in%20 US%20workplace&f=false

public sphere where the images constantly remind the audience of the "outsideness" of specific outfits and looks. It takes a certain amount of effort to overcome the attributions and eventually that can be achieved, but the initial steps are difficult because of the history and naturalized representations that circulate in the media sphere. The following shows the moments when these attributions are overcome, but that is not necessarily the case for most of the people from India who are aware of the attributions and are sensitive to the meanings associated with the clothes that are displayed on the Western screen:

> When Tiyash Bandyopadhyay moved to New York from Delhi and scored a high-paying job for a top-tier consulting firm, the then-24-year-old cut her hair in short layers and filled her closet with conservative suits. She didn't dream of wearing her colorful *salwar kameez* to work, though there were no explicit prohibitions against it in the company dress code. "Maybe it was my interpretation, but I felt there was an emphasis on people being all the same in terms of clothes and overall look," Bandyopadhyay says.
>
> Two years later, after she took a job as a product manager for a software firm, she read an article about Indra Nooyi, the Indian-born chief executive of PepsiCo, who once went on a job interview wearing a sari and sometimes attends company functions in one. ("Never hide what makes you," Nooyi has said.) Inspired, Bandyopadhyay began to integrate some of her traditional Indian pieces into her work wardrobe. "Nooyi got something that I had been missing," Bandyopadhyay says. "I dropped my pseudo-identity. By being myself—wearing Indian shirts and jewelry and talking about my holidays, like Diwali—I was more comfortable, so I could talk to people on an individual level rather than having this wall in between us." While several colleagues applauded Bandyopadhyay for her bold sartorial choices, most barely even noticed. "It really became a nonevent," she adds. "I only wish I had done it sooner."[10]

While the workplace is one of the spheres where the interactions happen, the other regime is the American neighborhood. As the Indians in the USA have achieved financial success, they have increasingly moved into the middle- and upper-middle-class

---

[10] http://www.marieclaire.com/career-advice/tips/a5805/ethnicity-in-the-workplace/

Image 8.4. Felicitating a Municipal Official at an India Festival in the USA

Courtesy: Author.

suburbs of America living as neighbors of the local population. It is here that some of the other interactions happen, and the interactions are often tempered by the images that circulate on the Western screen.

The Neighborhood

In February 2015, an incident that captured the attention of Indians across the world was the arrest of an Indian man, in his mid-50s, in a suburb of one of the Southern states of the United States. Historically, the states in the South that were on the confederate side of the American Civil War were known to be pro-slavery and thus, necessarily classed as more racist than the Northern states, at least, along the East Coast of the USA. Although the Civil War happened more than a century ago and there have been sweeping changes in American race relations, the undercurrents of racial intolerance continue in many areas in these States, as well as in other parts of the United States. But when an event occurs in one of the Southern States, it takes on a different color because of the histories associated with the states. The incident that attracted attention involved the arrest of an Indian man by two Caucasian police officers who manhandled the Indian man leading to life-threatening injuries and partial paralysis. The man who was arrested is the father of a diasporic Indian man and had come to visit the family. The person arrested was only in the United States as a tourist visiting family. The incident occurred in an upper-middle-class neighborhood—the very epitome of the American "community." This is precisely the kind of place where many superiorly mobile young Indian professionals want to live in as they move towards their American dream. Yet, it is in such as community that the matter occurred and it is useful to consider the event in some detail.

News reports indicated that the elderly Indian man, obviously a non-White, was taking a morning walk in the neighborhood. Curiosity drove him to stare at the homes that he was walking by. This behavior was noted by a neighbor, who remained invisible inside a house. The neighbor found the activities of the Indian man to be suspicious and reported the matter to the local police. The law enforcement authorities arrived quickly, made a

Image 8.5. An Indian Grocery Store in a Shopping Complex in the USA

Courtesy: Author.

failed attempt to speak to the person who knew little English, and then proceeded to throw him on the ground leading to injuries. The whole matter was captured by the video camera of the police car and the images later became available on the computer screen through digital social networks such as Facebook and YouTube. There are several aspects of this incident that are worthy of note in relation to the arguments I am making in this book.

First, attributions occur in many different scenarios, from the workplace to the neighborhood. These attributions are motivated, at least in part, by the images that one is surrounded by and in this case the image of a non-White person in the "safe" neighborhood is immediate call for concern since the images on film and TV have repeatedly shown how the colored "other" is always a cause for concern. The person who makes the call to the police is making the attributions which are "normal" under the circumstances of the lived conditions of the caller. This was a call to return "normality" to the neighborhood, which was being threatened by the "abnormal" intruder. There was perhaps no specific conflation of abnormality and being Indian, but it was sufficient to be an "other."

Second, the response from the police will be the point of much discussion and later litigation, but it remains the case that the police failed to communicate with the Indian man because of the individual's lack of knowledge and understanding of English. That, in itself, harks back to the brown-skinned person with little English that has been a dominant representation of the Indian. Whether the police recognized the person as belonging to the "model minority" or not will remain a matter of investigation, but the amount of violence used by the police was sufficient for the police department of the municipality to discipline one of the policemen involved in the incident. What remains in the case is that attributions were made, an action was taken, and victim of the police violence fit in well with the image of the Indian as shown on many different Western screens. These arguments might not point towards a direct relationship between the action of the police and the images on the screens, but there is a third element to the incident that does show that many in the "model minority" are suggesting that this incident is a part of a pattern of behavior towards Indians in many communities. Consider, for instance, the commentary reported in the leading Indian ethnic media outlet, *India Abroad*:

> Watching the video of Alabama police officer Eric Parker slamming Sureshbhai Patel to the ground, I internalized that concern immediately.
>
> And so did my immigrant mother, a retiree in Oklahoma.
>
> "Subodh, Beta, it's scary," she said. "It could happen to any of us, any time."
>
> As usual, my mother is right.
>
> And it has happened.
>
> In the last year, our legal system from Ferguson to Staten Island and from Florida to California has fumbled to address alleged police-brutality incidents. Too few desis, however, realize that these incidents far-too-often impact our own community.
>
> Consider a recent case our law firm handled in another red state.
>
> An Indian immigrant widow—a retired nurse and mom—was driving home after dark from worship at her Hindu temple, attired in a *salwaar kameez*. A plainclothes officer in an unmarked vehicle tried to pull her over, for no apparent reason. She was never cited for any traffic violation. Fearful for her safety, and concerned based upon rumors she had heard that this might be someone pretending to be a policeman, the woman returned the short distance to the temple.
>
> She knew the parking lot was well lit and that her fellow devotees would still be dispersing. As the woman left her car, the officer threw her—just like Patel—to the ground, shattering her knee into fragments. This left her bedridden for months, and has caused life-long pain.[11]

These reports provide strength to the argument that connections should be drawn between the ways in which the screens represent people from India and Indians and the way the people are treated outside India. Over time, a good number of these community events are based on attributions connected to the images.

---

[11] file:///C:/Users/Ananda/Downloads/indiaabroad20150227-dl.pdf

These are attributions that lead to different kinds of actions related to the way in which the minority in the diaspora is viewed by a segment of the local population, where the images on the screens have resulted in mistakes and misinterpretation with horrendous outcomes. The lack of understanding of a different culture and its intricacies are glossed over by the representations that are circulated on the different screens. Another way in which the conflation of different images happens is most evident in the case of the Sikh population amongst the Indian diaspora in the United States. Consider, for instance, the numerous attacks on Sikhs in the United States. The images of Islamic terrorism—personified by the turbaned image of Osama bin Laden—have resulted in situations where Sikhs have been attacked and killed by Americans who were focused on the image of the turban as the signifier of terrorists. For instance, in a *New York Times* report from 2012, it was stated:

> "I have been called Osama bin Laden walking down the street, because in the popular imagination a turban is associated with bin Laden and Al Qaeda," said Prabhjot Singh, who works in the high-tech industry near San Francisco. "But 99 percent of the people who wear turbans in the United States are Sikhs, so they face a disproportionate number of acts of discrimination."[12]

Instances such as this continue as the images play a role in defining Indians and India in the Unites States and elsewhere in the West. More recently, in the state of Washington in the North-West of USA, a temple was vandalized. As reported by Zee News,

> A temple in Washington was vandalized on the eve of its planned celebration of Maha Shivaratri.

> When members of the Hindu Temple Cultural Center in Bothell, 36 km from Seattle, went there on Sunday they found a swastika painted on it and "Get Out" scrawled in large letters with spray paint.[13]

---

[12] http://www.nytimes.com/2012/08/07/us/sikhs-mourn-victims-and-lament-post-9-11-targeting.html?_r=0
[13] http://zeenews.india.com/news/india/attack-on-hindu-temple-slur-on-us-name-congress_1548261.html

Other such events demonstrate the ways in which the India and the Indian are seen by some portions of the West, at least in the United States. Similar stories emerge from other parts of the West as well, where the Western screen continues to present the Indian as the "other" that does not belong in the West. It is, precisely, because portions of the audience see the otherness on the screen and are trained through a cultural and ideological process to treat the otherness as deviant and abnormal, exactly how the images represent the place and its people. This notion of difference carries on in other spheres of interaction as well where the second-generation of the diaspora, who are members of the country of adoption, also get treated in a particular way, precisely, because of the way in which their place of origin has been displayed in the media sphere. Consider, for instance, another communal space of interaction that is essential to most of the people in the West—the school or educational institutions across the United States.

The School

The Indian in the elementary, middle, and high schools of the West, particularly the United States, is often the second-generation diasporic. Their primary connection with India is through how they look, their parents, and the images they see on the various Western screens, including the satellite screen which often is the most viewed screen in an Indian household in America. This population of Americans comes in contact with the rest of the Americans as soon as they enter the day care center in America. These interactions are influenced by the images that both the groups encounter on the different Western screens. In the early days of the person's life, these interactions are influenced by teachers in the day care centers and kindergartens whose idea of India, and thus the Indian child, is often motivated by images that remind the teachers that the child comes from a non-English speaking home, because Indians do not speak English, as well shown on the Western screen. The child is often expected to be extremely brilliant for many screens that also show that Indians are generally very good in "studies," in particular, mathematics and the sciences. These are imaginations about the Indian, not only motivated by the screens but also through many other mediated mechanisms that inform the teachers about the culture of "model minority" in the United States even though the people have come from a place that is depicted in the ways discussed earlier in the book.

These imaginations lead to a set of interesting attributions made of the child and eventual behavior towards the child in the early days of the interaction in the schools. Consider, for instance, this slightly long quote from the work of Saran[14] who studies the condition of second-generation students of Indian origin in an American school and wrote,

> Rehana recalls her negative experiences in elementary school:
>
> We were always silent about many things that happened in school. In my fifth grade a white teacher called an African boy "Vermin." The same teacher did not like Indian children; she treated us like we were vermin. She did not like when I got the highest score in my class, or when I won the New York Times Poetry Competition and got a $12,000 award. She always shunned South Asian children in class and always ignored us. However, we never complained about this teacher. When my brother topped his class in fifth grade, his African American and Spanish classmates wrote a four-letter word in his yearbook. They wrote "you nerd we hate you"; "Stupid nerd I hope you die." We did not let our parents know about this because we knew they could not do anything to stop these things...and they would be worried. We did not report this to the school because we did not want to create more problems for us.

Rehana's story is typical of many Asian and Indian model minority students who demonstrate non-confrontational behavior and keep silent.

In many instances, this image of the Indian has been circulated on the different screens where the Indian has emerged to be the smart person and, therefore, automatically made into the "nerd" as often depicted in the media programs discussed earlier. An issue that is related to the way in which the second-generation

---

[14] http://www.krepublishers.com/06-Special%20Volume-Journal/T-Anth-00-Special%20 Volumes/Anth-SI-02-Indian%20Diaspora-Web/T-Anth-SI-02-06-067-079-Saran-R/T-Anth-SI-02-06-067-079-Saran-R-Tt.pdf

Indians respond to the different images on different screens is also connected with the core question of identity. The diasporic condition produces a set of crisis related to the questions of belongingness and the development of the sense of a self where the world external to the home of the diasporic offers a universe of discrimination. But the world internal to the second-generation children also becomes confusing as they relate to the images about India that are flashed across the screens of the West, now supplemented by the images brought home by satellite. To this unique, but rapidly growing, population of the second-generation Indians in America—the Indian-Americans—India is simultaneously composed of the images that show the place to be "abnormal" and "exotic," and the images that display the gyrations of the "item" dance played recursively in some of the music videos of the satellite channels. This confusion of images contributes to a sense of loss of identity that makes it especially difficult for this population to respond to some of the attributions they face in the world around them. The pejorative epitaph, American Born Confused Desi (Indian) or ABCD, reserved for the second-generation population becomes even more negative and palpable as the many images appear on the Western screen and people of Indian origin, who have no familiarity with India, begin to create images of themselves and the place of their ancestors.[15]

The "confusion" of the second-generation Indians in the USA is investigated in a study conducted by a graduate student, Laksmi Tirumala,[16] where she notes that the households with satellite images are often imbued with the images of India on the screen and the children are often surrounded by images that are quite different from the India that they encounter on the other

---

[15] The idea of the ABCD has been studied by scholars for some time as an indicator of the crisis of identity for people who are trying to create an identity narrative that retains elements of being Indian as well as being American. See http://scholarworks.gsu.edu/cgi/viewcontent.cgi?article=1005&context=anthro_hontheses and http://www.khabar.com/magazine/cover-story/gen_x_vs._gen_y_the_abcs_of_the_abcd_experience.aspx

[16] Laksmi Tirumala, "Bollywood Movies and Cultural Identity Construction among Second-generation Indian Americans" (MA thesis, Texas Tech University, 2009), https://repositories.tdl.org/ttu-ir/bitstream/handle/2346/18773/Tirumala_Lakshmi_Thesis.pdf?sequence=1

screens and in the attributions outside of home. The conflictual images add to the sense of confusion of identity where there is uncertainty about what it means to be an Indian in the USA. In the study the researcher noted, through numerous interviews with second-generation Indians, that the participants agreed and

> expressed that Bollywood is one of the better ways to learn about Indian culture and how they are being practiced in the society. This suggested that among different mediums, Bollywood movies in fact had the strongest influence on second-generation Indian Americans in learning and maintaining the Indian culture and traditions.[17]

While this is often true in the case of the second-generation Indians, it also points towards the kind of images that play a role among this population in imagining India and Indians. To be sure, not all of the images are authentic, and many of the images are internally contradictory—showing different faces of India on the satellite screen and DVD screens that bring these movies into the homes of this population. There needs to be a constant negation of the meaning of these conflicting images that eventually result in the conflict of identity where, much like the images of India on different screens for different audiences, the Indian-American, especially the second-generation, have to negotiate their identities for different audiences in the West who have differential access to the images. Friends of these youngsters are not watching the images brought by the satellite but are more familiar with the images brought by shows such as *The Big Bang Theory*, whereas friends of the immigrant parents are watching *Diya Aur Bati Hum*.[18] When the immigrant children relate to these populations, they are expected to be either Raj or Sandhya respectively. Yet, they are truly neither, and thus, they struggle to be something different, precisely, because these images have created expectations and produced attributions. This negotiation becomes a communal issue amongst the immigrants who started their lives in the USA at very early ages—some were born

---

[17] Laksmi Tirumala, "Bollywood Movies and Cultural Identity Construction among Second-generation Indian Americans" (MA thesis, Texas Tech University, 2009).
[18] http://www.hotstar.com/#!/diya-aur-baati-hum-81-s

here, others came here as infants. Indeed, the population is getting larger quickly and has led to a topic of discussion on Twitter under the name, "desiproblems"[19] that capture the issues of negotiation quite succinctly as demonstrated in some of the following tweets:

> Desi songs always come on the most when your white friends ask to hear your playlist. You're like ah wait…Fwd…Ah fwd

> If I had a dollar for every time someone spelled my name wrong

> You keep forcing your non-desi friends to watch Indian movies. You think they are awesome but they don't.

These and numerous other short posts begin to draw attention to the way in which the everyday life of second generation of Indians, as American as anyone else in the USA, are influenced not only the circumstances of their life but the images that inform the world around them about them.

Americans and other non-Indians witness numerous images as discussed in the earlier chapters that begin to offer an image of India and Indians. While these images are mobilized to understand the Indian in the USA or other parts of the world, the matter changes when the non-India is actually placed in India and surrounded by Indians. Again these images need to be accessed to negotiate their experience in India. The next chapter considers that experience when framed against the images of India on the Western screen.

---

[19] https://twitter.com/search?q=desiproblems&src=typd

9. THE WESTERN IN INDIA

I n the late 1900s and early 2000s, it used to be the case that the flights from America to India were populated mostly by the diasporic Indians travelling to India to visit family and friends, especially during the "holiday" seasons in either India or the USA. Parents would use the long summer vacations in American schools to take the family to India to introduce the American-born children to their Indian ancestors. Having lived in the USA for nearly 30 years now, I, too, remember well the ritualistic trip of going to *desh*, having done that particular trip nearly 30 times. The flights in the summers and winters would be predominantly populated by such people. Indeed, it was not uncommon to accidentally meet people on these flights when one would run into friends who too were diasporic and were making the ritualistic trip. For families with children in the West, it was also a time when the Indian families knew that they would have to prepare their homes for the invasion of the American grandchildren and their hyper-sensitive parents who would minutely examine every piece of food that

Image 9.1. Western Students Mingling with Students in a School in India

Courtesy: Author.

went into the mouths of the American children since the Western screen had reminded the diasporic of the horrid sanitation standards in India. As discussed in the last chapter, it is for these travelers that the mediated images of India became especially important as different generations of diasporic Indians would draw upon the imagery to negotiate their time in India.

There has been, over time, building up to the first quarter of the twenty-first century, an increase in another category of travelers who board these flights to India from the West. These are the non-Indians who are visiting India. It is, thus, not uncommon to see non-Indians at the boarding gates in London, Newark, and Frankfurt and getting ready for the adventure in India. Even casual observation would demonstrate that these are many different kinds of Westerners, from the young trekkers to the elderly couples, doing a conducted tour of Indian tourist destinations. In 2015, the passenger roster on the flights from New York, Washington, or Chicago would have a good many traditional American last names along with the Patels, Mitras, and Shahs. Indeed, as early as 2009,

Image 9.2. Western Students with Local People in the Himalayas

Courtesy: Author.

the largest portion of visitors to India was contributed by the US and the UK, and the number of visitors has constantly grown.[1] In a 2015 article in *The New York Times*, it was predicted that nearly 900,000 Americans will visit India in 2015 and India would be among the top 20 tourist destination for American coming next to Japan and China in Asia, but beating out countries like Ireland, Netherlands, Switzerland, and Australia.[2] It is a trend that can only increase as India also makes specific efforts to attract visitor

---

[1] http://articles.economictimes.indiatimes.com/2009-07-26/news-by-industry/28463291_1_business-visa-employment-visa-foreign-nationals
[2] http://www.nytimes.com/2015/01/11/travel/where-will-americans-travel-in-2015-.html?_r=0

from the West, particularly America, with emerging policies that allow travel to become more convenient with programs such as Visa on Arrival and with increasing flexibility of flights to India.[3,4] All the indicators, from the meetings between the heads of states to the increasing advertisements of travel to India in American magazines and newspapers, seem to indicate that Americans and Britons will be travelling to the place that has mostly appeared to them as images and narratives on the numerous Western screens discussed earlier. To understand how the Western screen could have shaped the experience, it is useful to begin by examining why they go to India and where they go.

DESTINATION INDIA

As I have discussed earlier in the book, starting in the early 2000s, the Government of India launched a program called "Incredible!ndia" that was designed to attract foreign tourism to India. It was a way to "brand" India as a destination where the tourist would be able to enjoy a specific form of the tourist experience, which would be unique and completely different from visiting other places. This effort was designed to work with private tour operators to promote an India that would look familiar to the foreigners and would mimic, in some ways, the expectations of the Western tourist who has experienced India through the Western screens, as discussed throughout the book. This India is made up of the exotic, the traditional, and often the "bizarre" that would make the place look like the images that have been produced and circulated in the West. It is evident in the series of video advertisements and print advertisements that have been commissioned by large advertising agencies. Most of the video advertisements, available in Internet-based video sharing tools, such as YouTube, have a set of common elements—the colors of Holi, the exoticness of locations in Ladakh, Rajasthan, a few images of the different ethnicities that a Westerner will encounter in India, people in traditional Indian clothes, and the Taj Mahal. No doubt, if one were to examine similar advertisements for other nations, some such motifs would be discovered. In other words, nations are often

---

[3] https://indianvisaonline.gov.in/visa/tvoa.html
[4] http://articles.economictimes.indiatimes.com/2015-04-09/news/60979664_1_upgrades-india-aviation-safety-rating-operations-inspectors

Image 9.3. Being Tourists in India

Courtesy: Author.

promoted based on what is "iconic" about the nation—the Statue of Liberty, the Great Wall of China, and the Pyramids. However, what is interesting about the advertisements directed to the tourists coming to India is the fact that what they see on media content of the Western screen is carried over into the advertisements produced by advertising agencies attempting to promote traveling to India. The traditional Western screen has exoticized India as I discovered in my earlier book and as I demonstrate in the analysis earlier in this book, and the "Incredible!ndia" campaign has tried to stay true to that image. It is not the case that the images highlight the icons only, but also stay congruent with the natural and "received" image that the audience of the Western screen would find familiar.

This alignment of the images and the "manufactured" reality for the tourist is also evident in the way tour packages are developed to simply highlight the specifics that the tourist can expect. Indeed, one of the taglines for the "Incredible!ndia" campaign has been "Find what you seek," yet much of the experience of the tourist is designed precisely not to seek, but stay within the boundaries of the images that they are familiar with. For instance, a 9-day tour package called Golden Triangle & Tigers offers the tourist a trip through Delhi, Agra, a tiger reserve, and Jaipur. These are all locations and elements of India that have been on the Western screen for ages and the tourist is treated to comfortable accommodation in these places and then returns with a confirmation that the images that they had expected to see are indeed what they saw and, thus, India is indeed what the Western screen has portrayed. There are numerous such packages that offer a luxurious experience for the tourist for the right prices, and reproduce the segment of India that has been the mainstay of the Western screen. In these cases, the tourist returns home convinced that India is indeed Incredible and very different from their home or their lives which go on untouched by India and continued to be shaped by the images on the Western screen and their "real" experience in India.

It is only when tourists stray from these paths, there is an opportunity to diverge from the images and begin to experience a sense of an India that has not been shown on the Western screen. Most of the times, such deviations from the screen-shaped path happen with repeat travelers who are no longer bound by the images that have permeated the screens in their Western homes. These are the tourists who are aware of the screen images and are able to recognize the distinction between those images and the India that presents itself to the traveler. Take, for example, the following statement from a traveler who has been to India many times:

> When I first started travelling in India nine years ago, the Delhi airport was basically a big, old shed and women almost universally wore swathes of fabric, in the Indian style. Now the Delhi airport is new and glitzy and could be in Houston; and many young women here wear jeans and t-shirts.
>
> In my own journey as an India traveler, I too am changing. When I first travelled in here, I was completely mesmerized by the novelty, and all the things about India that foreigners usually cite (colour, chaos, crowds, spirituality, historic sites, etc). I had a long and fruitful honeymoon stage. India was my muse, and I wrote thousands of words. But like all love affairs, it has become complicated.[5]

---

[5] http://breathedreamgo.com/2014/10/seventh-trip-india/

People who are open to these possibilities are the ones who are able to see the divergence between the screen and the reality of India. A tourist can later speak of the different experience in a flattering or derogatory manner, but at least these tourists experience a release from the narrative that is produced on the Western screen and reproduced in the tourist experience. I would argue that this release from the traditional narrative and the ability to offer and circulate an alternative narrative is an important development in the twenty-first century. I will get into this matter later in this chapter.

Tourists make up one of the key components of the Westerners coming to India, and they usually visit the predictable places and stay away from the everyday India that remains invisible to them. This is the India that goes to work every day, send children to schools, have servants to do housework, have a driver for the car, live in middle-class neighborhoods, have to struggle with a weak civil infrastructure, have to haggle over the price of potato in the local market, go to see movies at the multiplexes, and go out to the swanky shopping malls. This India is usually not seen on the Western screen, yet it is this India that is encountered by another category of visitors—those Westerners who come to India to work and study.

Some of the narratives and images on the Western screens have addressed the challenges faced by the people from the West who come to India for work. Movies like *Outsourced* and the corresponding TV situation comedy of the same name addressed the issue of travel in humorous ways. Especially, in the movie *Outsourced*, the narrative makes much of the "extreme" work conditions in India. The narrative revolves around the experiences of a young American man who is sent to India against his will to setup a call center. Using generic tropes such as "cow in the workplace" and "dysentery on arrival," the images and narrative offer an image that makes the Indian workplace distinctly different from the American office and shows the American worker the challenges of the place. The narrative offers an interesting closure which acknowledges the influence that India can have on an American single man, but it reaches that closure using a well-trodden road with all the pitfalls of working in India. Although the movie and the TV series were comedic, many of the themes encountered in other images were recycled, offering the consistent image of India that the Western worker in India can expect to encounter. Such images are important because the categories of Westerners who travel to India for work are different from the tourists.

Generally, the person who is in India for a job spends a longer period of time in India than the typical tourist, and the worker in India has to integrate a little more with the Indian way of life. It should be noted that there is an increase in the number of foreigners taking on the "expat" status in India where they leave their home country to spend extended amounts of time in India to pursue a profession.[6] An article in *The New York Times*, published in 2012, indicated that the number of work visas offered to Americans by the Indian Embassy in Los Angeles, USA doubled in one year between 2009 and 2010. The article went on to report similar jumps for parts of Western Europe as well.[7] These are people who come to India for work. Usually, they are relatively well-off and can afford to live comfortably in India. A majority of the workers live in metropolitan areas and have to "blend in" with the local ways of life in India. It is in the process of mingling into the culture of India that these sojourners begin to see the contradiction between the images that made up a significant aspect of what India meant before arrival to India and the India that the workers encounter.

The experiences of the expats, which are recorded in many different digital forums, offer a consistent view; the imagined India of the Western screen and the real India that they encounter are indeed different. This, however, can be claimed by any nation or group of people. What is on the screen is different from what one encounters when one is actually there. What is different in the case of India is the fact that the Western screens do not offer many alternatives, when indeed there are alternatives. The expat is often

---

[6] The term "expat" is the short for expatriate—a person who lives in a foreign country for an extended period of time to work in the foreign country. It is different from a diasporic immigrant since the expat almost always returns to the home country after spending an extended period in the foreign country. As such, an expat has little motivation to integrate into the culture of the country where the person works, as explained at the website called *Expat Info Desk*. Available at: http://www.expatinfodesk.com/expat-guide/what-is-an-expat/
[7] http://india.blogs.nytimes.com/2012/02/08/expats-flock-to-india-seeking-jobs-opportunity/?_r=0

nurtured on images produced by the tourist videos and films such as *Outsourced*. This is the primary representational resource available to the expats before they arrive into India. Furthermore, the screen has consistently focused on the narrative and textual elements described earlier that offer a relatively negative and exoticized image of India that does not usually do justice to the aspects of India that the Western viewer might find more "normal." The experiences of the expats begin to point toward these issues because it is a small group of people who have had the screen experience and the real experience. They begin to see the difference and are increasingly recording the difference with respect to some of the elements that have been consistently circulated on the Western screen as the exoticness of India.

Consider the element of food for instance; it has been the case that Indian food has been depicted as radically different from Western food suggesting that the Western person could be challenged by the Indian food, as is suggested by the screen images. Yet, the expats working in India offer a slightly different story as suggested in the following two statements:

> The food that was available was every bit as diverse as the food in the US but we generally stuck to Indian food because of the array of choices—given all the different cultures in India—was enormous, delicious, and quite healthy relative to the typical American diet[8].

> Western food is available, but you should be prepared to change your diet somewhat. South Indian food is flavourful, but not hot, but will def be more spicy than you'd get at home (think tex-mex if you're not experienced Indian).[9]

Both these statements hark back to the natural and accepted image of Indian food as being different from Western food, as well as, to the fact that Western food would be unavailable in India as is well-portrayed in many images, but the commentaries also offer an alternative image that is not usually seen on the Western screen.

---

[8]http://www.merinews.com/article/while-i-lived-in-gurgaon-i-never-wanted-to-leave-india/15864779.shtml

[9]http://www.expatexchange.com/ctryguide/4107/54/India/Expats-in-India-10-Tips-for-Living-in-India

For instance, in the film *Outsourced*, the protagonist takes a long taxi ride to find a place where he can eat a hamburger—a narrative strategy that continues to demonstrate the difficulty of finding Western food in India, whereas the following offers a different image, as stated by an expat:

> We lived in India with three kids who mostly wouldn't eat Indian food. I don't know the specific stores in New Delhi, but all large Indian cities have markets that sell international groceries, and the grocery sections in department stores now offer some western groceries and many Indian-produced products that are similar to western groceries. In New Delhi, you will also be able to find many restaurants that offer pizza, pasta, fast food, etc. They won't be exactly like what you're used to at home, but they will provide an alternative to spicy Indian food. You'll also find some common Indian foods that aren't too spicy that you and your kids may develop a taste for—rice & dal, breads, masala dosa, lassi, etc. We found we shifted our diet over to more fresh foods and less packaged foods. Fruits and vegetables are plentiful and inexpensive, especially compared to international groceries![10]

Similar inconsistencies can also be traced with other aspects of everyday life, such as practices related to the workplace and the culture of the workplace. The image of the Indian workplace does not show up too frequently on the Western screen except in some movies, such as *Outsourced*, but when it does, the workplace is represented as a very different environment from the Western one. The notions of time and punctuality are often represented as different, and this is the image that the worker takes to with them when they are expected to work in India. This, too, is a point of dissonance because the reality of the work culture that is encountered is different, and there are significant similarities with the West which is often comforting to the Western worker. For instance, in describing the work culture in India, one website, dedicated to supporting Western workers in India, states, "The corporate culture is similar to the West in its work processes and creativity.

---

[10]http://www.expatexchange.com/ctryguide/4107/54/India/Expats-in-India-10-Tips-for-Living-in-India

Office attire varies, though most workplaces expect formal or semi-formal dress, while certain organisations allow casual wear on occasion."[11] Similar statements can be found elsewhere the key point is that the environment encountered in India is not necessarily as distinctly different from the West as depicted by the presence of the cow outside the call center in the movie. The expat worker arriving in India with the cow image is often quick to realize that there are other alternative images that are often absent from the Western screen. It is also true for other categories of travelers.

While work has been a reason for Westerners to visit India for extended periods, another reason is beginning to emerge with the aging of the Western population, which is the decline in the quality of healthcare opportunities coupled with the rising cost of healthcare in the West. A new form of travel called "medical tourism" is beginning to emerge as the reason for travel to India. The US Center for Disease Control (CDC) describes the process as, "traveling to another country for medical care. It's estimated that up to 750,000 US residents travel abroad for care each year. Many people who travel for care do so because treatment is much cheaper in another country."[12] Indeed, as reports indicate, India is an increasingly popular destination for medical tourism because people from the West are increasingly finding affordable and high-quality medical care.[13,14]

In fact, the medical tourism becomes the premise for two Western movies, *My Best Exotic Marigold Hotel* and its sequel. In most of the cases, the people coming to India for medical treatment have little experience about India and their ideas of India are quite attenuated by the images on the screen as depicted in the movie. In this film, a set of elderly Britons travels to India for different reasons amongst which the medical need plays an important part. One of the protagonists is in India, represented in the colorful background of Jaipur, getting a hip replacement surgery because the wait within the National Health Services system in the

---

[11] http://www.expatarrivals.com/india/culture-shock-in-india
[12] http://www.cdc.gov/features/medicaltourism/
[13] http://edition.cnn.com/2009/HEALTH/03/27/india.medical.travel/index.html?eref=onion
[14] http://edition.cnn.com/2009/HEALTH/03/26/medtourism.interactive/index.html

UK would have taken too long. The narrative focuses on the initial anxieties of the travelers but closes with a representation of the travelers becoming permanent residents of the curious hotel, with one of the primary characters taking up employment in India to work in the ubiquitous and generic "call center" industry of India. A similar narrative is continued in the 2015 sequel where the protagonist integrates further into the fabric of India, becoming a part of an Indian space which is often not the focus of attention in the most of the images discussed in this book so far. Indeed, amongst the movies discussed in this book, these two movies actually do a more accurate representation of India, and especially, the medical culture of India that Western medical tourist's experience. In fact, one tour operator remarked:

> I was apprehensive about seeing this film: I'd heard it was cringe-inducingly stereotypical, but I was pleasantly surprised. I'm not aware of India being a place for retired Brits to live out their final years, as the characters do, but it's a brilliant idea. Not only are older people given greater respect in India, it's also normal for families to have live-in staff (my mother was born in India). Given the enterprising nature of Indian business, I can imagine a flurry of Best Exotic Marigold-style retirement hotels popping up all over the country.[15]

This statement applies to the specific movie, but overall the experience of Westerners who do medical tourism offers a different image of India compared to what is seen on the Western screen. The exoticness of India of the Western screen gets replaced by a more utilitarian India that is experienced with well-appointed hospitals, with doctors trained in the West, and with the facilities that could not have been imagined when finding India on the Western screen. These images come as a stark contrast to the images produced and circulated in the movies such as the *City of Joy* where the American doctor appears as the "savior" for the diseased people in the slums of Calcutta. Now, the savior is the medical establishment in India that is offering affordable care for serious ailments of Americans. The apprehensions that are produced by images

---

[15] http://www.theguardian.com/culture/2012/mar/04/tour-operator-best-exotic-marigold

of India in many of the movies about India, as discussed here, disappear and a different India comes into view calling into question the conventional images. This change in the perspective on India becomes more crucial as the process of medical tourism has been gaining popularity, and in 2012, *The Huffington Post*, a Web-based newspaper, did a series of stories on medical tourism. I use the quote below to demonstrate the difference between the India on the Western screen and the possible experience of the viewers of that image when they travel to India. Consider the following:

> The JCI-accredited hospital at which Schuler was treated—Fortis Hospitals in Bangalore, India, formerly known as Wockhardt Hospitals and is associated with Harvard Medical International—exceeded his expectations.
>
> "They picked me up at the airport at 4 a.m. their time and took me to the hospital" for X-rays, Schuler said. "My room was incredible, the care was phenomenal. I was there in the hospital for seven days and I was in what I consider to be a four- to five-star health facility."
>
> "When they rolled me into surgery, I remember looking at my doctor and saying, 'If it's not successful, just let me go,'" Schuler continued. "He said, 'It'll be ok.' By 8 a.m. I was under the knife and by noon they got me up and I was pain-free. I could not believe it."[16]

Such reports call into question the attributions a traveler would make to India and Indians based on the images of India on the traditional screens of the movie theater and the TV. However, as discussed in this book, there are newer screens to consider and newer images to examine, especially with the way in which these newer images are impacting the Western traveler, and the way in which the traveler is recreating and recirculating an image of India on the newer screens of the computer as discussed earlier. It is useful to consider the "gap" between the traditional image, the experience of the traveler, and the possibilities of representation that arise out of the gap.

---

[16] http://www.huffingtonpost.com/2012/06/04/medical-tourism-health-tourism-medical-travel_n_1551217.html

THE TRAVELERS' INDIA

There are many different reasons for which people from the West would travel to India and for the different reasons, they go to different places. Some would only be to the "tourist" places, others would be at the workplaces of India, and some would see only the inside of a hospital. For all of these travelers, the experiences are different from each other and the image of India offered on the Western screen becomes of little use in negotiating their time in India. The images, primarily on the TV and movie screens, provide an unproblematic and monolithic view of India that contradicts the images obtained by the travelers.

One of the most important outcomes of the travel experience is the dissonance between the experience and the expectation. As discussed here, there is the potential for a vast mismatch between what the screen had predicted and the actual experience. The formula of the screen is unable, and perhaps unwilling, to keep up with the emergent reality of some parts of India, which the formula cannot incorporate into the image. The image must remain true to a generic narrative and representational style that will ensure popularity to the vast number of viewers in the West.[17] The image does not have to cater to the small segment of viewers who would actually travel to India for any reason. Given that only about half the population of the US holds a valid passport to travel outside the US; the image makers are not specifically concerned with the tiny portion of Americans, for instance, who could "question" the image based on the experience of travel abroad. There is no compelling reason to alter the course that has been established on the Western film and TV screen. Indeed, such digression from the formulaic reality could prove to be dangerous at the Box Office when India is no longer what the viewer expected it to be.

---

[17] The notion of "genre" is particularly important here. The idea of genre refers to an unwritten contract between the audience of an image and the producer of the image. Over time, the audience is trained to recognize certain traits in a narrative that classify the narrative into a category or genre, and offers the reader the ability to interpret the narrative because it appears similar to other narratives of the same genre. Thus, a Western cowboy from Hollywood must incorporate the horse just as a contemporary Bollywood thriller must have an item song. These formulaic representational elements make a film "generic."

Yet, travel is increasing and there are more people who are experiencing the gap. In the days before the explosion of digital communication technologies, the gap was just recorded in the personal journals of the travelers and described at dinner conversations about the travels to India. It is now changing as there is greater access to the narratives of the travelers on other screens, for instance, the computer screen that was discussed earlier. It has been in Chapter 6, the computer screen offers Indians an opportunity to reinvent and represent India in a way that is not consistent with the images on the institutional screens of the West. The same practice continues with the traveler who often would share the images and narratives on the non-institutional screen which is, nevertheless, very globally accessible. These narratives often find their way, through the digital grapevine, into media spaces where the "other half," without the passports, would also encounter the alternative narrative and images on the computer screen. This is of particular importance because these narratives that appear on the computer screen are no longer authored by Indians, but by the Western person who has experienced India and the gap between image and reality.

When India is imaged on multiple screens, this particular image on the computer screen has some interesting implications. The representations now are produced by people of Western origin and meant for the computer screen of the Western audience producing, often, a counterpoint to the images on the traditional screen. For instance, there are now specific Web logs (blogs) about travel in India. One such notable blog is called *Breathedreamgo*. "Breathedreamgo was launched on August 23, 2009 and it has grown over the years to become one of the top two 'India travel blogs' according to Google search." In December 2014, Breathedreamgo was ranked 59 on the list of Top 100 Travel Blogs and in April 2014, one of the Top 50 Travel Blogs by *The Expeditioner*. Here are Breathedreamgo numbers as of November 2014:

Google page rank: 4
Unique visitors per month: 32,000
Page views per month: 68,000

Twitter followers: 15,300
Subscribers: 2,500
Facebook friends on all pages: 8,000
Breathedreamgo is also on YouTube, Flickr, Google+, Pinterest, Instagram
Visitors come from (in this order): India, USA, Canada, United Kingdom, Australia and Germany.[18]

A Web presence such as this offers a different image of India as stated in a brief blog,

> [I]n a small village, on the edge of nothing, I found myself on a rooftop with dozens of women in their best saris, holding their babies, waiting in line to have me take their photo for the first time. And months later, when I returned, we all sat on that same rooftop, giggling over the photos I had brought them until it was dark outside. Sisterhood.[19]

This is precisely the presentation of India that begins to fill the gap between the traditional representation of India on the Western screen and the images encountered by travelers from the West. As shown in this chapter, there is increasing evidence that the images and the representation of the lived experiences differ from each other. People in the West, who become interested in India, now have different screens to turn to in order to prepare for India and Indians. The significance of India on this particular Western digital screen is the fact that these representations are produced by people who are not of Indian origin. The authors are people who were surrounded by the traditional images but began to experience something different when in India. Although this has been true for generations, there never was a screen that was so accessible to the author and the reader that would facilitate the filling of the gap.

Furthermore, unlike the institutions that have had control on the Western screens, with the obligation to monetize the image and make a profit from the formula, the individuals who start their

---

[18] http://breathedreamgo.com/about-breathedreamgo/
[19] http://breathedreamgo.com/2015/03/25-reasons-to-love-india-travel/

blogs are often motivated differently. The bloggers often write with the genuine pleasure of recording and sharing their experiences. The owner of the well-known blog, referenced earlier, started the blog as a result of a trip to India. The trip itself was motivated by the need to overcome certain tragedies, but in describing the process of blogging, the author says,

> I have written probably a half-million words about the effect that trip had on me. How it gave me back my dreams, recharged my life, made me feel I was finally home and provided me with the inspiration to finally start my writing career. I had wanted to be a writer since childhood, but I didn't have my subject matter until I went to India.[20]

A different India begins to show up on the Western computer screen, especially for the ones who are seeking to find information about India and are ready to venture beyond the generic and widely accepted images that are available to the Western audience. It creates a set of openings for recreating India for the audiences of the Western screens, calling into question the conventional images that circulate in the West. The alternative images offer an internally contradictory representation where the "monolithic" India is no longer the only image available. This questioning of the conventional has become critical and much more accessible now than what it was when the main outlets of the images were on the movie screen as I have examined in my earlier book. The institutional Western lens is no longer the only way to look at India. The changes in technologies and the changes in the way India has become central in the global sphere is making these "other" images increasingly important. In the next chapter, I summarize what India looks like today on the Western screen and what the story of India appears to be on the different screens.

---

[20] http://breathedreamgo.com/2012/01/write-and-blog-about-travel-in-india/

10. THE INDIAN NARRATIVE SCREENED

E arlier in the book, I made references to the idea of a story or a narrative. Humans are sometimes considered to be "narrative beings"—entities that tell stories, listen to stories, and make sense of the world around them through stories. Consider the most fundamental of stories that are narrated in an elaborate answer to the simple question, "Where are you from?" That question is extremely provocative—with narrative potential—many stories could be told as an answer to the question, and each of the stories would paint a different picture of the place of origin of a person and the person himself or herself. The response to the question becomes a narrative identity, and many conclusions can be drawn from the stories that make up the response.

In many cases, different stories would be told in response to such a question. For example, as an immigrant to the USA, when I am asked that question in the USA, it is possible to say something to the order of "originally from India, now from North Carolina." However, when I am being asked the same question in India, I could simply say "from Calcutta" and that would be a believable story although technically inaccurate. This relationship between believability and accuracy is especially important in the case of this book. In my case, the first answer is the most believable and most accurate response. The color of my skin would make it less believable that I am from North Carolina. The precedent "originally from India" makes the story believable and eventually accurate. On the other hand, if I offered the response as "from North Carolina" when asked the question in Delhi, the believability is somewhat less because at first sight I would not be mistaken to be from America. Thus, the most accurate story would not necessarily be believable, whereas the believable story "I am from Calcutta" would remain so even though it is inaccurate. There can be numerous similar examples of the process where there is an awkward tenuous relationship between believability and accuracy.

This awkwardness can be connected to the story that the listener is expecting to hear. The expectation is the product of acculturation—the way in which something is expected to be—an obviously Indian looking middle-aged man is expected to be from India, not North Carolina. When the expectations and the stories match, there is a sense of "static"—things are as they should be. It is often this desire for static and the desire to "not raise additional questions" that stories are manufactured to match the expectation and uncontradictory stories which are believable, though inaccurate, become the way people present themselves. One important aspect of this process of storytelling is the fact that the people construct and circulate their own stories. These become tiny autobiographies as opposed to biographies that are constructed by others. In the personal telling of the story, the storyteller maintains a sense of control or agency. As such, the storyteller can choose different stories, even if they are contradictory, to meet the needs of specific circumstances.

This sense of agency disappears when stories are narrated by others. Then it happens to be that the subject of the narrative loses agency, and others are able to construct the narrative at their will to suit the purposes of the narrator. Those purposes are manifold, and in the case of media institutions, it is often the case that the institutions attempt to retain a sense of static and provide the audience what is "expected" in order to remain popular. In doing so, it is often safest to construct a believable narrative even though it might not be accurate. A good example of this aspect of storytelling by media is witnessed in stories of some specific places. Consider, for instance, a film that would be set in Egypt. It would almost always be the case that the pyramids and the Sphinx would be featured standing in the majestic desert and ostensibly far away from the humdrum of everyday life. This is the believable story. Yet the accurate story is the fact that the Sphinx stands in the middle of the crowded city of Giza. And a few hundred feet's walk from the Sphinx, across a busy thoroughfare, are some multinational eating places such as Kentucky Fried Chicken (KFC) and McDonalds restaurants. Depicting the real image would go counter to the attempt of creating the uncontradictory and monolithic image of Egypt. A similar process was discovered in my analysis of movies about India when I wrote my earlier book. In that analysis, it was shown that the agents of the narratives—Hollywood—created a relatively uncontradictory narrative about India that was more believable than accurate. India was viewed through the Western lens and the same India was seen every time the Western lens was pointed at it.

Now, when looking for the story of India on the Western screen, a different story emerges. The monolithic narrative is replaced by a more complex narrative where the different screens tell different stories—which often contradict each other. One of the primary reasons for this contradiction is the emergence of different agents—storytellers—who are all bringing the story of India on the Western screen. In closing, it is useful to consider different aspects of this contradictory story of India that emerges on the Western screen.

THE TALE OF MANY INDIANS

The history of the Indian subcontinent would demonstrate that the region has been built around a set of contradictions with many different forces impinging upon the region, creating a variety of cultural and everyday practices that defy the attempt to create a single story of India. This diversity of India is well known and documented within India, and people in India grow up with the diversity. Even middle-school books on history and culture remind

Indian children of the diversity within India, and an Indian in India is well aware of the internally contradictory aspect of India and being Indian. Yet, to many of the outsiders who have tried to tell the story of India, there has always been an attempt to find a set of elements that would allow a simple telling of the story of India where the diversity is replaced by finding the most believable story that a specific audience would expect. That attempt has failed over and over again. From the works of Rudyard Kipling to the advertisements enticing foreigners to come and visit India, the various attempts of creating the "narrative of India" fall apart as soon as a foreign visitor enters the country. For instance, I have, over the past several years, brought young American college students to India. And when they come to India, without fail, they are always struck by the fact that this is not what they expected. The expectations based on the stories are almost always contradicted since the monolithic stories fail to capture the contradictions.

It is only now, as described in this book, that the myth of a single India is being called into question as different Indias are beginning to show up on various Western screens. These different Indias are represented in a large range of practices which include the segments of the traditional story of India with its exoticness and mystery, but that is quickly being supplemented by other representations such as the India of multinational corporations or the place to reach out to when facing challenges of high-school geometry. Some of these narratives simply did not exist in the past. New developments in the technology, new forms of education, and new demands in the West is allowing the creation and circulation of narratives that can become confusing because of the distance of the narrative from the expected and "believable" narratives about India. Consider, for instance, the stories about India that would describe it as the destination for "medical tourism," which is a polar opposite to the stories of India that would present it as an overpopulated country where mysticism and magic take the front seat as compared to science and technology. These contradictory stories raise a series of concerns about the representation of India on the Western screen and the reality of India that interacts with the rest of the world.

One of the outcomes of this change is the fact that there is a divergence between the representations of India on the Western screen. By and large, the traditional screens continue to offer the believable stories to meet the expectations of the audience, often choosing to ignore other authentic narratives which would not be believable. However, that gap is now been filled by the multiplicity of screens that are narrating the story of India. It is no longer the case that the authentic narrative which tells the story of an emerging global power is now absent from the screen. As I have shown in this book, these narratives are increasingly accessible to the Western audience and, therefore, are challenging the traditional narratives which gained the position of "authenticity" mainly because there were no other narratives available.

A second outcome of the creation and availability of the multiple narratives, most of which are authentic, calls into the question the identity of India on the Western screen. The gradual replacement of the traditional believable monolithic narrative makes it increasingly more difficult for the viewers of the Western screen to pinpoint what India is like and what they might expect from an Indian. It is no longer just the country of snake charmers and maharajas; it is also not just the country where large corporations outsource jobs; indeed, it is a country whose hallmark is indeed the combination and coexistence of many different practices that defy the attempt to be corralled into a single "Indian narrative." It is a place which can only be represented through many different narratives, some of which could easily contradict each other, making it especially difficult for the audiences of the Western screen to understand what India is. It becomes most evident when visitors from the West are unable to find their imagined India and realize that there really are many Indias. The Western screen has just begun to represent these various Indias, and with time, it is possible that the many different Indias will actually be seen on the Western screens, offering a complete representation of India.

The complete representation will eventually be of benefit for both the West and India as India becomes a more important player in the global system. Perhaps, the most important impact of that more well-rounded representation will be on the exchange of people between India and the West. Most indicators suggest that this exchange will only increase over time, and it would be imperative that the complexity of India be better represented and understood in the West. It would help establishing the inevitable interactions between the people more effectively, with the Westerner better understanding India and Indians, without having to rely on uncontradictory and incomplete representations that used to be the case in the past. For the people of the West, it will be important to go beyond the India that was seen through the Western lens of the 1900s and create a composite image that is increasingly being depicted on the Western screens.

EPILOGUE

THEORETICAL FRAMEWORK

Much of the work presented in this book rests on the theoretical and methodological positions developed by a large range of scholars, and, in this glossary, I provide indicators to the primary bodies of work that I have drawn upon.

To begin with, it is useful to place this work under the umbrella of cultural studies. The project of cultural studies began in Europe primarily after World War II when European scholars turned to the thinking of Louis Althusser (1918–1990) and Antonio Gramsci (1860–1937).[1] They noted that the notion of culture needs to be understood as material practices of different segments of people with the understanding that there are specific ideological positions inscribed within the practices. At any

---

[1] Antonio Gramsci, *Selections from the Prison Books* (New York: Lawrence and Wishart, 1982).

moment in time and space, there is a specific set of practices that become the dominant practices of the culture at the expense of the practices of the subordinate groups. This disparity is accompanied by the sense of struggle—sometimes called hegemonic/ideological struggle—where the subordinate engage in questioning and eventually upending the struggle when alternative practices take on dominance and practices of the culture tend to shift. This theoretical position was expanded upon by the pioneers of cultural studies such as Stuart Hall (1932–2014) and his cohort at the Birmingham School of Cultural Studies. Their project was to engage in a careful discursive and narrative analysis of the media and ethnographic studies of the audience, as pioneered by cultural anthropologists such as Clifford Geertz (1926–2006), to understand the role of media in shaping culture as seen in the work of David Morley and Charlotte Brundson.[2]

It is those methods that are applied in the analysis provided here. These methods focus on the actual text and the discourse of the audience to engage in an analysis which considers the texts from a semiotic perspective as suggested by Roland Barthes (1915–1980), Claude Levi-Strauss (1908–2009), and Ferdinand de Saussure (1857–1913).[3] All of them suggested that it is possible to find specific patterns of codes and signs in texts that offer a meaning which is not available to the surface level of the text. However, by taking the text apart, it is possible to see the ways in which text and narratives are constructed by looking at, for instance, the narrative codes and functions as suggested by Vladimir Propp (1895–1970).[4] It is also possible to look at the visual and aural elements of the text, as suggested by John Fiske, to see how the text is internally connected and interconnected with other texts to produce the specific meaning within a cultural context.

The analysis in this book has also relied on the notion that narratives make up a significant part of the human experience,

---

[2] David Morley and Charlotte Brundson, *The Nationwide Television Studies* (London: Routledge, 1999).

[3] Ferdinand de Saussure, *Course in General Linguistics*. Eds. Charles Bally and Albert Sechehaye. Trans. Roy Harris (La Salle, Illinois: Open Court. 1983).

[4] Vladimir Propp, *Morphology of the Folk Tale* (Austin, The University of Texas Press, 1968).

and as humans, we perform as "narrative beings," suggested by Walter Fisher. I use this notion to suggest that the many textual elements of the different media discussed here offer a story about India, which is internally inconsistent where the different narratives elements engage in an ideological struggle to constantly retell and reproduce India on the Western screen.

However, the fact that a nation, or its people, can indeed be imagined through mediated narratives is suggested in the work of Benedict Anderson (1936–2015) at the theoretical level and is applied to a group of people—Orientals—in the work of Edward Said (1935–2003). These scholars offer support to suggest that mediated images become a key tool in imagining people and places that the audience has never experienced in the real life. Usually, the dominant ideological position is reflected in the narratives and it becomes the "work" of the subordinate to create the space to find the alternative voices and alternatives as suggested specifically in the works of Homi Bhabha and Gayatri Spivak when considering the imaging of India and Indians in the global cultural space.

I would encourage the interested readers to engage with the work of the scholars mentioned here by starting with the following seminal texts.

INDEX

ABOUT THE AUTHOR

Ananda Mitra is a Professor of Communication at Wake Forest University, teaching courses on new media, India, and research methodology. His publications include a 10-volume series on digital technology and its social impact, a critical examination of the Indian TV series *Mahabharat*, an examination of the portrayal of India in the Western cinema, a book about the ways in which new digital technologies are increasingly alienated from the users, a book on the cultural issues surrounding the use of social media, and two books on research methodology. Some of these include *Digital DNA: Social Networking and You* (2014), *India through the Western Lens: Creating National Images in Film* (SAGE 1999), *Alien Technology: Coping with Modern Mysteries* (SAGE 2010), and *Television and Popular Culture in India: A Study of the Mahabharat* (SAGE 1993).

He has consulted with many different industries and is the inventor of the concept of "narbs" that allows for a careful and systematic narrative analysis of the unstructured component of big data that has become available with the growth of social media. He is considered a specialist in analyzing the way in which narratives produce images of people and places, with a special emphasis on representation of Indians across the globe.